# DELICIOUS GEOGRAPHY

# DELICIOUS GEOGRAPHY
## From Place to Plate

*GARY FULLER AND T. M. REDDEKOPP*

ROWMAN & LITTLEFIELD
Lanham · Boulder · New York · London

Published by Rowman & Littlefield
A wholly owned subsidiary of The Rowman & Littlefield Publishing Group, Inc.
4501 Forbes Boulevard, Suite 200, Lanham, Maryland 20706
www.rowman.com

Unit A, Whitacre Mews, 26-34 Stannary Street, London SE11 4AB, United Kingdom

Distributed by NATIONAL BOOK NETWORK

British Library Cataloguing in Publication Information Available

Library of Congress Cataloging-in-Publication Data Available

ISBN 978-1-4422-4532-7 (pbk. : alk. paper)
ISBN 978-1-4422-4533-4 (electronic)

∞™ The paper used in this publication meets the minimum requirements of
American National Standard for Information Sciences—Permanence of Paper
for Printed Library Materials, ANSI/NISO Z39.48-1992.

Printed in the United States of America

# CONTENTS

# ABOUT THE AUTHORS

**Gary Fuller** is professor emeritus of geography and population studies at the University of Hawaii. He is the author of the award-winning book *The Trivia Lover's Guide to the World: Geography for the Lost and Found* and was a winning contestant on the television program *Jeopardy.* He lectures about geography aboard cruise ships and resides with his wife, Barbara, in Kailua, Hawaii.

**T. M. Reddekopp** is the wife of Jim, mother to five children, and grandmother to one (so far). They moved their family from the burgeoning island of Oahu to the rural slopes of Mauna Kea on the island of Hawaii to begin a vanilla farm and business in 1999. She has infused vanilla into things most people won't dare to, and together they have created experiences to share vanilla with the world. Today, they host more than 10,000 visitors a year on their farm and at their Vanilla Experience Luncheons. She still prefers chocolate ice cream over vanilla if given the choice. You can find her at www.hawaiianvanilla.com.

# ACKNOWLEDGMENTS

*Dedicated to a visionary, a kind, loving gentleman who was a huge part of our lives, Jim Reddekopp Sr. (1926-2015). Dad or Grandpa or Pops. We miss you.*

**Dr. G's**: Barbara Fuller, wife and mother of the authors, provided both editing and pictures. She also provided encouragement, without which this book would never have become a reality.

This book would never have seen the light of day had it not been for Chef T's steadfast perseverance in the face of difficulties that I felt were insurmountable. She found the way out, and I am grateful. I have worked with other coauthors but never with one I admired and loved more.

**Chef T's**: This book would not have been possible to do without the unwavering support, love, and constant encouragement from my family. This book was written during one of the most difficult and beautiful years of my life, and to be pushed to complete something I had begun was not an easy task. I am eternally grateful to my husband, Jim, who is truly the Brave Hero in my story. Ian and Malia and Aria—you bring me such joy each day, you really have no idea. Emma—my dearest girl, my gift, and magical creature, I am sure I couldn't have done this without you. Isaac—your loyalty, commitment to our family and willingness to pursue difficult things makes me so proud and brings me wealth beyond measure. Elliot—your ability and skill level to adapt amazes me; my Virtuoso, don't ever lose your *charisma.* Aidan—your steadfast strength and calming, loving presence in my life warms our home. I love you all tremendously. You are my greatest wealth and most valuable treasure.

This book *really* would not have been possible without the enduring, constant support from my mother, Barbara. She worked to edit, produce photos, proofread, compile, taste test, listen to us complain (especially at 3 o'clock on Christmas Eve). Mom, you are amazing.

And for my Dad, who had the idea in the first place . . . you are a rare gem. Thank you for this opportunity.

# DR. G'S PREFACE

*"The gentle art of gastronomy is a friendly one. It hurdles the language barrier, makes friends among civilized people, and warms the heart."*

—Samuel Chamberlain

What has geography got to do with food? A whole lot, I think. During the first two decades of my life, I did not, nor did anyone I knew, ever eat bagels, enchiladas, escargot, or Stilton cheese. None of us had ever heard of hummus, sushi, or kiwi fruit. Wine was never served with any meal I ever ate. The expansion of dietary choices is a wonderful example of the reunification of mankind. After millennia of dispersal, we finally settled the last frontier, New Zealand and the deep Pacific, and have been re-meeting ourselves for at least the last five hundred years. We now share food from many places, created in the contexts of cultures new to us. Geography is charged with the task of describing, analyzing, and predicting aspects of this coalescing of humanity and providing the survival tools necessary. Food and, especially, food security are crucial aspects of this task.

Our curriculum may need updating. At present, a geography curriculum commonly includes the spatial distribution of cultural aspects of mankind; language and religion are favored topics. Maps are used to show, for example, where French and Chinese are spoken and where Islam and Christianity are the dominant creeds. Agriculture is also a feature of the basic geographic curriculum, and we often refer to regions of the world by the staple grains they produce. East, South, and Southeast Asia, for example, share rice cultivation in common, even though languages differ sharply across the rice-growing regions. Seldom, however, does geography delve into the finished product, food, as an object of study. The rice crop may be similar in Japan, Korea, China, India, parts of Africa, Mexico, Louisiana, and California, but the foods derived from the common crop are certainly quite different.

When geography considers cultural factors, it almost always considers language first—and it should. Language strongly unifies people who share it, and strongly separates them from those who speak a different language. Language thus produces regions and boundaries between those regions. Put another way, language is strongly impressed on the landscape and can be mapped. No other cultural facet so unifies (and divides) people as language does. People will give up many aspects of their culture, but will likely surrender their language last.

If language is the most enduring of our cultural makeup, what comes in second place? Many might say religious beliefs, and perhaps that is so, but in our contemporary world, I would argue for food preferences. There are many examples of wholesale religious changes throughout history. The expansion of Buddhism, Christianity, and Islam to the point where at least a third of the world's population follows these creeds is proof of the alteration of religious beliefs. The Edict of Fontainebleau, issued by Louis XIV, provides another interesting example. Louis demanded that Huguenots, French Protestants, convert to Roman Catholicism. History books often report the devastating effect this had on France's economy because some Huguenots, who were successful entrepreneurs and craftsmen, fled the country. What is less frequently reported is that most Huguenots did, in fact, convert.

I suppose we can argue today that France is predominantly Roman Catholic, but I suspect France is actually predominantly indifferent to religion (although many of its immigrants are certainly not). At the same time, it seems inconceivable that France would give up its daily purchase of baguettes, or consumption of cheese, wine, or café au lait. Culture is always being modified, of course, and just as "le weekend" has crept into French language, so McDonald's has modified the French cuisine.

Regardless of how we rank food in the order of cultural importance, it remains an important feature of the world's cultural mosaic. Because geography has almost entirely ignored food, it has been left to others—cookbook authors, for example—to write about the effect of all kinds of environmental factors on our food. Good cookbooks often turn out to be excellent geographic primers, even if the focus is only on the narrow matter of food.

Strangely, while geographers seldom publish articles on food, it's always surprised me how many geographers have taken an avocational approach to food. Two leading lights of modern geography, the late Harm de Blij and Peter Gould, studied wines extensively. Several of my colleagues at the University of Hawaii also took a passionate interest in foods—everything from British cheeses and New Guinea "spinach" to coffee production—but none of this interest made it into print in their research publications. This book, then, may be a pioneering effort to bring food into the geography curriculum.

# CHEF T'S PREFACE

**ge·og·ra·phy**

jēˈägrəfē/

noun

noun: geography

1. The study of the physical features of the earth and its atmosphere, and of human activity as it affects and is affected by these, including the distribution of populations and resources, land use, and industries.

## THE GEOGRAPHY OF COOKING

Cooking for me is very much about a sense of place. The comforting confines of my familiar kitchen with all of my tools and equipment in their given places, my *mis en place* (French for "putting in place") for preparing a meal—my recipe either in my head or in print—is all like being on a ship, with me as captain, directing where we will go, with my recipe as a map of sorts. I am in command of the destination—will we have a spicy Indian curry or a comforting casserole? Will this be for a picnic or a candlelit dinner?

Cooking is also about feeling. Almost every week I ask my family, "What do you feel like eating?" Food evokes memories. It is important for me to pass on traditions that evoke meaningful and special memories. Food is helpful with understanding our roots, our values, and how we show our love. Traditions are a way of coming together in agreement in so many ways.

Cooking is about learning something new about a people or a place. Food can transport us to a foreign land, and our palate is the doorway. A perfect new tradition to start is conversation that teaches—one that it is not just about satiating our stomachs, but our minds and souls as well. This can be a new tradition that builds a bridge of understanding between cultures—food, fellowship, good conversation, and open minds and hearts are all that you need to cross borders that have once been closed.

It is then also important to practice the art of hospitality and not treat the traditions as exclusive, but inclusive. To be included in such celebrations year after year creates vivid memories and bonds that tie you to a sense of place. When we open our home and lives, and the sharing of our traditions and food, we are giving a gift beyond measure. It allows others in to see how our family truly operates.

When I was growing up, it was natural in our home for my father or mother to ask questions of what we knew, and for them (as teachers) to share their knowledge. We all had busy work and school schedules with many different interests and extracurricular activities added in, but I still remember dinners or gatherings where we would discuss everything from baseball (my dad is a huge fan) to travel (yes, we were quizzed regularly on capital cities, where mountain ranges and rivers were located), to movies and pop culture (my dad could never keep up with the current fads, so we kids were always happy to speak on something he was less familiar with!).

A lifelong love of learning is what this has instilled in me. We chose to homeschool our children, and they are all incredible self-learners. Growing up in the age of the internet has opened up learning opportunities that have never before been available, and this has afforded them some incredible opportunities and also, unfortunately, some incredible distractions. However, dinnertime is one of the most important times for all of us and still holds a place of priority.

Tonight, all my children (including my daughter-in-law and grandbaby-to-be) will be home for dinner. I made double-chocolate almond butter cookies, a hearty beef stew, and basil potato salad. I can't wait for the conversation and learning that will happen—even if it is just learning about how my family members spent their week.

Cooking is very sensory and artful. It can be vigorous (canning, baking twenty-four loaves of Challah for holiday gifts), relaxing (making handmade pasta and three sauces to go with—pesto and shrimp, roast garlic white sauce, rustic meat and tomato—Andrea Bocelli is on the stereo, good wine decanted, and lots of laughter), or just routine (quick dinner before a performance/soccer game/meeting).

Cooking is about planning. What I have found is that when I don't take the time to prepare or really think through our schedule and shop efficiently for what to feed myself and my family, I tend to make bad choices and then end up feeling like cooking is a chore rather than savoring the entire process. This requires an awareness, a willingness, and slowing down. It also is a choice to take the time to make preparing, shopping, and mealtime a priority.

\*    \*    \*

Taking the time to go to the farmer's markets and getting fresh produce is something I love to do. Living here in Hawaii, most of our produce is shipped or flown in from the contiguous forty-eight states—what we call "The Mainland." It is a shame, because if there were a little more effort, we (as a state) could be growing a lot more to become more self-sustaining instead of being extremely dependent on the transportation industry.

When I was growing up on Oahu, my dad tried his hands at cucumbers and tomatoes, and I remember his love of roses. Our family has always had a few small areas (in addition to the greenhouses and shadehouses where we grow vanilla) where we grow produce. Today, as I write this we have Swiss chard, pole beans (which we had two nights ago—delicious), onions, broccoli, cauliflower, tomatillos, chervil, and leeks; plus our lemon trees are fruiting, avocados are falling off the tree across from the mill, and we have an herb and lettuce patch. We have two Duroc hogs and eight chickens. Wherever you are, you can, with very little effort, create your own small garden—even just a pot of fresh herbs brings life and freshness into your home and cooking.

We try to be good stewards of the land, and we are always learning more. I don't know if we can ever do enough, and I sometimes wonder why these things are not taught more in the schools today. Our home is a completely off-grid solar home with a generator for backup. We have really good water from the county and our water is solar heated. We are getting better at recycling, and if you have ever received a package from us, we reuse all of our incoming packaging supplies to ship things to you. I am trying to use fewer things in plastic packaging and be aware of my usage of it. We have all used reusable water containers for years to help cut back on the millions of plastic water bottles that are used each year.

My desire for this book is to be a map for you to begin your own journey of exploration into the wonderful, diverse world of food— and for you to open your hearts and minds to new cultures, flavors, and, perhaps, learn a few things along the way with the trivia questions my dad has thoughtfully prepared. Food for thought, if you will, just for you.

## MY METHOD

This means that I have described the way that I make all of these recipes in my kitchen. A lot of these recipes have been made many times over many generations, but again, this is my method. Last year, I completed my Master Food Preservers certification, and there were many Best Practices that go with canning and preserving, ones that are there for our safety. There are many Best Practices within everyday home cooking as well. Once you know the basic kitchen rules about sterilization, preparation, and food safety, cooking becomes unmuddled—you are free to work within these parameters. You will develop your own Best Practices and hopefully use these recipes again and again as I do.

Your most important tools in the kitchen are your hands and your common sense. Be an explorer, be creative, be bold—but also temper that with extra thought to flavor combinations, the salt quantity in all ingredients before adding more, fat content and quality if you are watching your diet, and temperatures of food before, during, and after cooking.

There are so many ways to cook and to make a recipe your own. Never be constrained by my way of making something—feel free to add or take away, adjust or tweak to your liking. Letting go and not being hindered by too many rules is what makes being in the kitchen a truly enjoyable experience.

Chef T says:

Flour is always all purpose unless I say otherwise. If the air is humid, clumps will form in my sugar or flours, so I will push it through a sieve and sift it. This is especially important with powdered sugar, cornstarch, baking soda, and baking powder.

Sugar is always granulated unless noted otherwise.

Butter for baking is always unsalted, but I add salt to the recipe.

Salt is always kosher salt.

I am writing these recipes for the home cook—meaning that I am expecting you to know your equipment and how they operate, especially your oven (and its geography, such as where its hot spots are).

I live in a solar home, and being energy conscious, I wait to preheat my oven until I am sure I am ready in about 15–20 minutes to put something in. I also will often turn my oven off for the last 10 minutes or so to allow something to finish cooking, especially when baking bread, cakes, or cookies. This not only saves on fuel, but allows a more natural cooling process to begin in the oven, rather than the drastic temperature fluctuation of pulling something very hot into a cool room.

EVOO—Rachel Ray is the first person I saw use this—stands for extra virgin olive oil (brilliant and time saving when writing!). I always buy the best quality I can afford. I had the privilege of visiting one of the oldest family-run olive oil farms in Spain, and good olive oil is worth every penny.

When you can, source local and buy these first. Support the farmers in your area.

# THE SEARCH FOR SPICES

*Question 1: What valuable spice did Vasco da Gama bring back from India?*

*Question 2: What country did Pedro Álvares Cabral accidentally discover on the way to India?*

*Question 3: Where did cinnamon originate?*

*Question 4: What spice did Ferdinand Magellan's fleet bring back that paid for the entire voyage?*

*Question 5: How do you make Old World Meets New World Spiced Wine and Malabar Pepper Gougères?*

Did our teachers lie to us? Columbus was a great hero, or so they taught. Now he is widely condemned by Native American and other groups for bringing European exploitation and disease to the Americas. In our home state, Hawaii, he has been struck from the calendar: no more Columbus Day. This is not fair to Columbus or the other explorers. For thousands of years, mankind had been moving to the far corners of the globe. Like cockroaches and rats, we learned to live in an enormous range of habitats; that was our key to survival and eventual dominance of the planet. In our separation, we developed new languages, new belief systems, new foods, and even new physical characteristics (minor, but noticeable). It was inevitable that we would reunite someday and that, when we did, the differences we had developed were going to cause big trouble. Don't blame Columbus for the inevitable!

But did those teachers deceive us about what Columbus was really up to? He wasn't trying to prove the world was round. With the possible exception of a few congressmen, everyone has known the world was round for a long time, a time well before Columbus. He wasn't trying to find a New World. In fact, he never believed he had found one, but even after four voyages, he still thought he had been to Asia. True, he was trying to find a shortcut to the East Indies (modern Indonesia), but he was actually on a suicide mission. He thought the world was much smaller than it actually is. Just about everyone else, probably including his ships' officers and maybe even common seamen, didn't agree with him. If he had actually been able to sail on an uninterrupted path to the East Indies, he would have run out of food and water before he got even half way there. Our teachers did say something about spices, but the message up front was that the Spanish were motivated by Gold, God, and Glory. While these three Gs fairly described Spanish colonization in the New World, the early voyages were all about spices. Maybe your teacher and textbook said that—mine didn't.

Spices were in great demand by European gentry at the time the explorers began their voyages. They trickled into Europe through well-established routes to Asia. By sea, the Romans had sailed to India and, before them, so had the Egyptians. One of the Pharaohs was buried with peppercorns in his nostrils. Cloves, which came at that time only from a tiny area in the Molucca Islands, were used in Syria in 1500 BC. They came by land as well—in fact by several routes, of which the legendary Silk Road was one. Why did Europeans at the time prize spices? This is akin to asking why people buy and drive $100,000 cars. I doubt they were really needed; after all, Europeans had many seasonings for food, including saffron, grown in Spain, and we have Fords and Chevys. Because they were prized and envied, spices were not worth their weight in gold—some, including cloves and nutmeg, were worth much more than that.

The Portuguese figured out that if they could sail to India, they could cut out all the middlemen on the spice routes to Europe and make a fortune. Under the leadership of Prince Henry the Navigator, the Portuguese began making voyages down the west coast of Africa. Gradually, they extended their range, until finally Diaz reached the Cape of Good Hope in 1490 and Vasco da Gama sailed across the Indian Ocean and reached the Malabar Coast in 1498. Vasco da Gama landed at the large trading port of Calicut (now Kozhikode) and was asked why he had come. His answer: to find Christians and spices. Both were there: the Malabar Christians may be the oldest Christian congregation extant (then and now), and black pepper is native to the slopes of the Western Ghats Mountains on the Malabar Coast. At that time, and well over a century later, it was immensely valuable. *Da Gama may have brought other spices with him, but black pepper was the prize!*

After da Gama returned, both he and another Portuguese spice-seeker, Cabral, were determined to make more voyages to India. Cabral, having learned how difficult the passage around the Cape of Good Hope was, decided to swing far to the west to pick up favorable winds and attain the proper sailing angle to round the Cape. *He went so far to the west that he discovered Brazil and claimed it for Portugal.*

Cabral and da Gama bombarded Calicut and other nearby areas and claimed the entire spice trade for Portugal. They were never able to control the spice trade fully as there were too many traders and too few incorruptible Portuguese in the area. Although the Malabar Coast was a long way from the Spice Islands, where the real riches were, the Portuguese controlled enough of the spice trade to enrich themselves. In addition to pepper, they also attempted to control the cinnamon trade. *Cinnamon is native to Sri Lanka* (earlier, Ceylon), but there is a near relative, cassia, that was grown widely in Asia. Cassia, much cheaper than cinnamon, was traded in Europe, but cinnamon was preferred there, just as it is today. In the United States, real cinnamon is becoming more available, but most of the product sold as "cinnamon" in the United States is actually cassia—and it's cheaper than real cinnamon.

The Spanish and the Portuguese had agreed in the Treaty of Tordesillas to divide up the world between them. A line of longitude was selected in the Atlantic; Spain got everything to the west of the line, Portugal everything to the east. That meant Portugal got the spice trade with India. By 1520, the Spanish knew for sure that their "New Spain" was not near the Spice Islands (despite Columbus's assurances) and that no spices had been found in the New World. Hmm, is it possible—the Spanish thought—that the treaty line extends all around the world and that, on the other side of the planet, the Spice Islands are actually on our side! Even better, since longitude could not be well measured on shipboard, no matter which side of the line the islands actually are, we can always fudge it a bit. So they got a Portuguese captain, Ferdinand Magellan, five Spanish ships, and a crew and set out to find a way to the Spice Islands, just as Columbus originally tried. Magellan needed a route through the New World and, fortunately, looked to the south, where he found a strait (eventually named after him) and, a month later, sailed into the Pacific.

Magellan was killed in the Philippines, but his crew, having no idea where the Spice Islands were, simply asked people along the way, and eventually found them.

Of the five ships Magellan started with, only one, the *Victoria*, survived, along with fourteen of her crew. The ship arrived in Spain in tatters, and investors who came to see it must have been disheartened. *The ship's hold, however, contained enough cloves to pay for the entire first 'round the world voyage and produced a small profit besides!* At the time, no one really cared about the fantastic accomplishments represented by the voyage—there also seems to have been little concern about Magellan. The cloves, however, were another matter!

The recipe below is meant as an appetizer. Mulled wine was common in the Age of Exploration, perhaps because so much of the wine was of poor quality!

# From Geography . . .

*Caribbean island (photo by bbf)*

# . . . to Gastronomy

*Spices in a market (photo by bbf)*

~

Food for Thought:

*"I cook with wine, sometimes I even add it to the food."*

—W. C. Fields

~

## Recipes for:

Old World Meets New World Spiced Wine
Malabar Pepper Gougères

# MULLING SPICE MIX

This makes 1¼ cup of mixture, which can flavor the **Old World Meets New World Spiced Wine** recipe. You can also package it up in cheesecloth or small muslin bags in two tablespoon amounts, tie it up with some baker's twine, and give as a lovely hostess gift or a take-away for a party.

## INGREDIENTS

½ cup whole cinnamon broken into pieces or chips

¼ cup dried orange peel

¼ cup whole cloves

¼ cup whole allspice berries

1 vanilla bean, scraped (reserve pod for your sugar bin, honey jar, or homemade vanilla extract)

10 star anise, optional

10 whole cinnamon sticks, optional

## MY METHOD

Combine all ingredients in a bowl, making sure the vanilla gets evenly distributed.

Store in an airtight container.

If giving as gifts, add one star anise and one cinnamon stick to each bag.

# OLD WORLD MEETS
# NEW WORLD SPICED WINE

A perfect recipe for a chilly winter's night. You can use apple juice or cran-apple juice instead of the cider, but if you can find cider, I recommend it. It adds a rich flavor. You can also omit the wine altogether, making this a family-friendly, festive refreshment. This is another perfect recipe for a gathering since you can make it ahead of time. I think you will truly enjoy the way the vanilla notes will soften any bitter edges and make this a new favorite.

## INGREDIENTS

1 bottle (750 ml) Cabernet Sauvignon
4 cups cider or juice
¼ cup vanilla honey (if you have it, if not, use regular honey)
2 tablespoons mulling spices
Juice and zest of one orange
*Cinnamon sticks and star anise, for a nice garnish

## MY METHOD

Combine all ingredients in a heavy-bottomed pot. Bring to a boil. Reduce heat to low and simmer for 10 minutes. Strain into a serving pitcher. Pour into mugs to serve and add a cinnamon stick as a garnish.

***Make ahead:*
This can be stored in the refrigerator for up to a week.

*Old World meets New World spiced wine (photo by bbf)*

# MALABAR PEPPER GOUGÈRES

*Makes about 6 dozen bite-sized appetizers*

Basically a simple *pâte à choux* recipe, these delectable bite-sized puffs are a perfect accompaniment to drinks served during cocktail hour.

The freshly cracked black pepper welcomes a warm and spicy note on the palate, while the cheese brings a nutty creaminess and slight saltiness that complements this old world spice.

## INGREDIENTS

1 cup whole milk

1 cup water

1 teaspoon granulated sugar

2 teaspoons salt

½ lb. unsalted butter

2 cups plus 2 tablespoons all-purpose flour (sifted)

9 large eggs, at room temperature

2 cups grated Swiss or Gruyère

2 teaspoons freshly cracked Malabar black pepper

## MY METHOD

Heat the oven to 350°F. In a large saucepan over medium heat, combine milk, water, sugar, salt, and butter.

When the butter is fully melted, stir in the flour with a wooden spoon.

Stir for another minute or so over low heat, to release some of the moisture in the dough, until the dough pulls away from the edges of the pan.

Remove from heat and allow to stand for a minute.

Either by hand or with a stand mixer, add in the eggs, 3 at a time, incorporating each batch before adding the next.

Stir in cheese and black pepper, not over mixing, until just combined.

Pipe or mound by tablespoonsful onto parchment-lined sheet pans, allowing at least one inch between each mound.

Bake at 350°F for 20 to 25 minutes, until the gougères are golden brown and toasted.

***Make ahead*

These can be made ahead and frozen for up to 2 weeks. I will place them in the freezer on a baking sheet to freeze and then put in an airtight container.

Pull out as many as you need, thaw, then reheat at 350°F for 5 minutes or until crisp.

# MARCO POLO TRAVELS EAST

*Question 6: What was Marco Polo's native land?*

*Question 7: Who was the ruler of China during Polo's visit there?*

*Question 8: What monetary system, unknown in Europe, did Polo observe in China?*

*Question 9: What fuel, also unknown in Europe, did Polo describe?*

*Question 10: Who imprisoned Polo after his return home?*

*Question 11: How do you make Spinach and Vanilla Rice Casserole?*

Before Diaz, da Gama, Columbus, or Magellan, there was Marco Polo, who planted the seeds for the great geographic discoveries in the Age of Exploration. My impression is that most of my students think marco polo is only a game played in a swimming pool, but I have a special affinity for the real Marco Polo, a Venetian trader who visited the court of *Kublai Khan* in the thirteenth century. Many people did not believe stories attributed to Polo when he *returned home to Venice*, and this doubt has continued down through the centuries. By strange coincidence, when I returned from doing research for my PhD in Chile, I also had many doubters about stories of my experiences. Polo did not see all of China (although he may have been the first European to see the Pacific Ocean), and I did not see all of Chile.

China, perhaps more than any other place and civilization, has experienced remarkable ups and downs. At least once in the past, and perhaps several times, China had the world's largest economy,

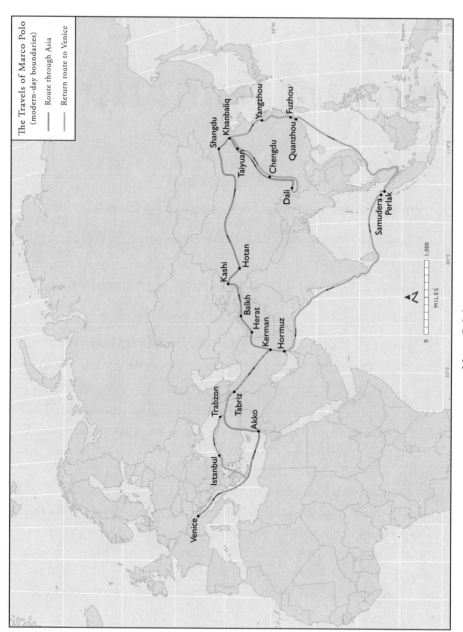

*Marco Polo's route*

but after achieving this, the economy collapsed, due to foreign invasion, depopulation, and major emigration.

Subsistence rice cultivation, dominant in China's agriculture, may be the most important of all agricultural types in terms of the number of people it feeds. There are competing claims as to who developed this agricultural type and where it began. The first geography course I ever took adamantly insisted that the Yangtze River valley in China was where it began. The second course was equally insistent that Korea invented rice cultivation. The latest evidence, however, indicates rice cultivation first occurred in the Pearl River valley of China, at the end of the last Ice Age.

Dr. G. says: Korea has a climate particularly favorable to double-cropping of rice.

About a thousand years before Marco Polo visited China—roughly 200 BC until 200 AD—the first great boom period happened. This was at the time of the Han dynasty, generally considered the period from which modern Chinese draw their identity. It appears that, while the Han Chinese did grow rice, it was not then the dominant crop it was to become. Polo, since he traveled to south China, encountered rice, but I doubt he found much in the court of Kublai Khan. Contrary to the American stereotype of the Chinese as rice-eaters, rice was not grown in north China. Rice is a preferred grain because it yields more nutrition per unit of land area than any other commonly cultivated grain. Rice cultivation has been pushed north in recent decades, probably mostly due to new varieties of rice that require a shorter growing season, and perhaps also due to the influence of climate change.

The Polo family—Marco's uncle and father were with him—had a harrowing return journey, which involved sailing around the Indian subcontinent. When they finally got back to Venice, they had a great deal of wealth in the form of precious jewels. They returned, however, while Venice was at war with Genoa. Marco entered the war, apparently as a sailor, and *was captured and imprisoned by the Genovese.*

Marco Polo did not, as far as we know, write an account or diary of his twenty-four-year journey to China (or to "Cathay" as it was known in Europe), but while incarcerated, he told a fellow prisoner about his experiences in China. While we have no definitive original manuscript, the story of Marco Polo's experiences in China was published and circulated widely in Europe. Polo's adventures, what we might call an early geography, apparently stimulated a great interest in cartography for centuries to come. Fra Mauro, who lived two centuries after Marco Polo, was a well-known Venetian cartographer. While I cannot say his famous map of the world was particularly accurate, it was certainly a beautiful work of art.

Dr. G. says: A bonus trivia question: Where is the Fra Mauro crater and associated rock formation? It is on the moon and, in fact, was the destination of the ill-fated Apollo 13 expedition.

The information Marco Polo brought home with him was both valuable and interesting. Polo witnessed *the Chinese using paper money,* an unknown practice in Europe at the time. Polo also observed *"rocks" being used for fuel; while Europe's industrial revolution five hundred years later would be fueled by coal,* it, too, was apparently unknown at the time.

Other things attributed to Marco Polo are not true. One common trivia question involves the invention of spaghetti. China had made noodles, mostly from millet, rather than wheat, for perhaps a thousand years before Marco Polo arrived. Italy, however, had spaghetti before Marco's time. Did someone else bring the idea from China to Italy before Marco Polo? Probably not. Some also credit Marco Polo with bringing back the idea of home furniture. While there's no question that the Chinese crafted beautiful home furniture, Europeans also had furniture long before Marco Polo was born.

What about ice cream? Since Nero had frozen desserts made from Alpine ice a thousand years before Marco Polo, no one wants to credit Marco with bringing gelato to Italy. While the Chinese did not invent ice cream, they did make it, and, yes, Marco Polo did bring the idea home with him.

Marco Polo's report of an ocean to the east of China caught Columbus's attention. That the world was round was common knowledge among both sailors and educated people in 1492. Where there was some disagreement, however, was about the circumference of the earth. Columbus thought the world was about half the size it really is. He visited the Azores, the westernmost point that Portuguese and Spanish navigators had reached. One can imagine that Columbus envisioned Marco standing in China just over the horizon from the Azores.

Were it not for the imprisonment, we would have never heard of Marco Polo—and I presume kids would play christopher columbus at the pool.

# *From Geography . . .*

# *. . . to Gastronomy*

~

Food for Thought:

*"Without rice, even the cleverest housewife cannot cook."*

—Chinese Proverb

~

## *Recipes for:*

Spinach and Vanilla Rice Casserole
Vanilla Rice

# SPINACH AND VANILLA RICE CASSEROLE

*Serves 8*

Rice is a staple in Hawaii and is served with almost everything. Our kahu (pastor/teacher) tells the young men in our congregation not to marry a woman unless she knows how to cook rice—white rice—in a pot on a stove. This is the only way I knew how to cook it when I got married because that was how my mom made it (although she does serve it with butter, which is a big "no-no" in Hawaii). Imagine my dismay when my husband asked me to make rice in a rice cooker. His friends were all coming over, and I didn't want to disappoint him by not using the rice cooker he bought (and I wanted to appear adept at all things in the kitchen!). I read the instructions and put the rice in, added water, and pressed the button. Well, I didn't know that there was a steamer attachment in the bottom that completely messed up the cooking of the rice and made a big, gloppy mess. I ended up driving quickly to the Safeway down the street to get rice—because rice is served at every meal. Today, I only make rice on the stove top. I have learned that it truly is an art to know exactly how much water to add to get just the right plumpness in the grains—not scorch the bottom or make mushy rice. Rice should have enough starch to cling together so that it can be picked up with chopsticks—the reason you should not add butter, which makes the grains separate.

This casserole is one of my boys' favorite meals—you can make it with brown rice (which we have been making more of since one of our sons was diagnosed with diabetes this year) or a mixture of the two. Basmati rice is also a nice, nuttier-in-flavor substitution.

*Spinach and vanilla rice casserole (photo by bbf)*

## INGREDIENTS

1 Portuguese sausage, quartered and diced

1 large onion, diced

8 cups cooked Vanilla Rice (recipe follows), cooled

4 pkg. boxed, frozen spinach, thaw and squeeze the water out until very dry

8 eggs, lightly beaten

2½ cups whole milk

2½ cups shredded cheddar & jack cheese blend

1 teaspoon dried thyme

Corn flakes, crushed (optional)

## MY METHOD

**This can all be done in one pot—so use a large one to accommodate all of the ingredients.

Fry the sausage in a large pot. When nicely browned, drain on paper towels and wipe out the pot to remove most of the grease. Then add onion and sauté until translucent and softened.

Add the rest of the ingredients and stir until well combined.

Pour into a well buttered (or vegetable sprayed) 9 × 13 baking dish. Top with crushed corn flakes and gently press into the rice mixture.

Bake at 375°F or until the top is nicely browned and all moisture is absorbed, about 30 minutes.

**We serve ours with a hot sauce like Frank's or Tabasco.

# VANILLA RICE

The butter is added in this recipe to help disperse the vanilla seeds—vanilla uses the fat to blend with the other ingredients.

## INGREDIENTS

4 cups white rice
4 tablespoons butter
2 teaspoons kosher salt
Vanilla seeds scraped from ½ of a bean

## MY METHOD

Measure out rice into a heavy-bottomed pot that has a tight-fitting lid. Add warm tap water to the rice and, using your hands, sift through the rice to release the talc. Carefully dump that water out, using your hand to keep the rice grains from slipping through (you can also use a fine-meshed sieve, and then place the rinsed rice in your pot). Wash-rinse-repeat two more times. Pat rice down so that it is even in the pot. Using your pinky finger as a guide, place the tip of your finger on the top of the rice and add warm tap water until the water comes up to the first knuckle line on your pinky. Place the pot on the burner and bring to a low boil. Add butter, salt, and vanilla and give it a quick stir. Cover and lower heat to the absolute lowest setting and cook for 20 minutes, or until the rice is fully steamed, all of the water is absorbed, and the grains are soft (brown rice will take about 10 minutes longer). You can check to see if it is done by using a wooden spoon or spatula to scoop to the bottom of the pot and see if all of the water is absorbed, or to pull a few grains out to taste, but cover again quickly because you don't want to lose too much of the steam from the pot.

# A PLANT IS DOMESTICATED
# IN BOLIVIA

*Question 12: What are Bolivia's two capitals?*

*Question 13: What city is at the mouth of the Seine River?*

*Question 14: What country lost population over the years 1860–1960 but is now the fastest growing country in Europe?*

*Question 15: What county in the lower forty-eight states is closest to Europe?*

*Question 16: Where was the potato chip invented?*

*Question 17: How do you make* **Pommes Frites** *with Garlic and Vanilla Aioli, and Colcannon?*

The agricultural revolution is among the most important of mankind's accomplishments, but it is often misunderstood. It is not really a sudden "revolution" since it began thousands of years ago and is still underway. It is also not the idea of planting seeds in the spring and harvesting crops in the fall. The core of the agricultural revolution is the domestication of plants and animals and, specifically, selective breeding to change species so as to make them more beneficial to people.

In understanding what selective breeding has done, it is useful to compare dogs and elephants. We know from DNA evidence that all dogs had wolves as their ancestors, but when we compare Chihuahuas with Great Danes, it is easy to see the influence of selective breeding. Asian elephants, used by people as beasts of burden for thousands of years, have remained largely unchanged: elephants have been tamed, but never domesticated. Could we use selective breeding to create elephants that were bigger or smaller? Perhaps, but it has not been done.

*Bolivia is distinctive in the Americas because it has two capital cities: La Paz and Sucre.* Bolivia is also the home of the potato. This is the tuber that Americans call the Irish or white potato (although it can be several colors). It is distinct from the sweet potato, native to Central America, or the yam, native to Africa. Amerindians in Bolivia developed hundreds (perhaps thousands) of varieties of potatoes, some of which were also grown in Chile—99 percent of all present-day potatoes are derived from the Chilean varieties.

> Dr. G. says: Bolivia is also distinctive because it is the only country in the Americas that is truly landlocked, that is, without access to an ocean. Paraguay also lacks a coastline, but it's on La Plata River and therefore has access to the Atlantic.

Although early Spanish explorers took the potato back to Europe, it was not grown by farmers to any great extent until the eighteenth century. Because it grows underground, the potato escaped the various diseases that frequently ravaged grain crops. It could also be grown on land that was marginal for other crops.

Although the potato has become a staple in the diets of several national groups, no national group has taken to it more ardently than the French. The French fry (*frite*) is commonly served with all kinds of restaurant fare—it is no surprise that Americans named the treat after France. The British, avid consumers of the same product, call it a "chip" probably because, as a matter of principle, they would not name anything after the French. On a recent trip to Paris, I dined

*Bolivia's two capitals*

in a restaurant that specialized in mashed potatoes; I suspect it may be unique in the world.

*I first visited Le Havre, France, at the mouth of the Seine River in 1960.* Despite the passage of fifteen years since the end of WWII, Le Havre still displayed much war damage; it may have been the least attractive city I had ever seen. I visited again in 2014—the transformation of Le Havre was nothing short of miraculous. Instead of war damage, I saw a rebuilt city with award-winning design and architecture. In the restaurant in which I dined, frites were served with every dish on the menu!

The white potato is associated with Ireland more than any other country. By the 1840s, Irish peasants had become dependent on the potato (a variety known as the "Irish lumper") to an incredible extent. Male Irish workmen might consume as many as sixty potatoes a day, with wives consuming about half that number. When the potatoes in Ireland were struck by a blight, a huge famine developed almost immediately. So severe was the famine that the Irish were said to have died from the "green mouth disease," meaning that people were found dead along country roads with their mouths stained green as they attempted to eat grass and weeds.

*Ireland continued to lose population throughout the nineteenth century and the loss continued until 1960. Since then, however, Ireland has gained population to the point where it is the fastest growing country in Europe, with an annual growth rate of around 2 percent.*

Potatoes are grown in many parts of the United States and were a staple of dinner most nights, not only in my home when I was growing up, but in the homes of all my friends as well. My father would often buy a large quantity of potatoes at roadside stands along the south shore of Lake Ontario. There, the soils were formerly the lake bottom and were as black as ebony. My mother was disdainful of these inexpensive tubers and called them "muck potatoes," which they truthfully were, but her tone implied there wasn't anything worse. On occasion, mom would buy Maine potatoes. The bags said they came from Aroostook County, Maine. *Aroostook County is famous for potatoes, but during World War II, someone in the war department must have been a geographer and figured out that this was the county (in the lower forty-eight states) closest to Europe.* While the Air Force base there was not completed until the war was over, Aroostook's location meant that, for several decades, it was defense jobs, rather than potatoes, that were the staple of the economy.

Dr. G. says: Aroostook County is a traditional part of Acadia (see chapter 7). There have been attempts as recently as 2005 to make all or part of the county part of New Brunswick, Canada.

If the shelves of my local grocery store are reliable witnesses, the potato chip must be the most popular American snack. In any case, they generate more than $15 billion in revenue annually. Where did they come from? Although there are competing stories, *the potato chip was probably invented in the mid-nineteenth century in Saratoga Springs, New York,* by a cook named George Crum. The product was marketed, at least in upstate New York, as the "Saratoga Chip"; my grandparents always used that name for them (but never bought them!). The British (as usual) have a different name for the potato chip; they call them "crisps."

# From Geography . . .

## . . . to Gastronomy

~

Food for Thought:

*"What I say is that, 'If a man really likes potatoes,*
*he must be a pretty decent sort of fellow.'"*

—A. A. Milne

~

## Recipes for:

Pommes Frites with Garlic and Vanilla Aioli
Colcannon

# POMMES FRITES WITH GARLIC AND VANILLA AIOLI

*Serves 4–6 as an appetizer or side dish*

One of the great benefits of working with different chefs is learning the variety of ways they prepare dishes. I have learned to "double fry" my frites to get that desired texture of tender-on-the-inside, crispy-on-the-outside. I have also learned that excess moisture in anything you are frying will cause a soggy end product. Make sure to take the extra steps if you want truly stellar frites. I hope you enjoy the aioli as much as my family does—when we run out, there is much disappointment. The vanilla adds a soft mellowing of the garlic, rounding out the vinegar in the mayonnaise. Pair this with the frites as well as the **Sweet Pepper and Onion Jam** from chapter 14—wonderful together on a crusty slice of bread.

For the frites:

## INGREDIENTS:

5 lbs. russet potatoes
½ cup tapioca flour (you can also use corn starch)
EVOO or vegetable oil for frying
Kosher salt

## MY METHOD

Wash and peel potatoes. Cut into thin slices, about ¼ inch thick. Stack slices and cut again forming sticks. Have a bowl of cold tap water ready and put cut potatoes in to allow some of the starch to release. Soak for at least 30 minutes and up to one hour.

Drain the potatoes in a colander and spread them out onto a paper towel lined baking sheet. Allow moisture to draw from the potatoes for at least 30 minutes, using paper towels to press excess moisture out. Place potatoes in a brown paper bag (or large bowl) and toss with tapioca flour, making sure to coat all of the frites.

In a large stock pot, heat 2 inches of oil to 360°F. Fry ¼ of the potato sticks at a time. Fry until they just form a crust, 2–3 minutes, and then remove with a wire skimmer or slotted spoon. Spread them out onto another paper towel lined baking sheet. Allow the oil to reheat to 360° F before adding the next batch.

Frites can be prepared ahead up to 4 hours to this point in the process. When you are ready to serve, heat your oil again and fry the frites a second time, working in the same batch size. They should turn golden and crisp within 2–3 minutes per batch. Remove with skimmer or slotted spoon to fresh paper towels and sprinkle with kosher salt. Serve immediately with aioli.

# GARLIC AND VANILLA AIOLI

*Makes about 2½ cups*

## INGREDIENTS

10 garlic cloves, peeled and thinly sliced

3 tablespoons EVOO

2 cups best quality mayonnaise

1 teaspoon garlic powder

Vanilla seeds scraped from ½ bean, reserving pod for
   another use

## MY METHOD

In a small skillet, heat olive oil to medium-low and add garlic. Sauté garlic for 4–5 minutes, stirring often until garlic is softened and beginning to brown—I will cover the skillet to allow them to steam a bit, which allows the garlic to soften better. Remove from heat and allow this to cool completely.

In a large bowl, combine mayonnaise, garlic powder, and vanilla seeds.

When garlic and oil have cooled, add into mayonnaise and stir well to combine. Allow at least 30 minutes for the flavors to meld before serving; it's even better to make it the day before. The aioli will keep covered in the refrigerator for up to 10 days. It goes wonderfully with artichokes, grilled meats or fish, and, of course, the frites. Enjoy!

# COLCANNON

*Serves 3–4 as a main dish, 5–6 as a side*

This is my version of a very simple, comforting dish—creamy leeks, sharp kale, warm potatoes, and crisp bacon. You can make it ahead for a Sunday brunch—serve it with a poached egg, sour cream, or a sprinkling of sharp cheddar, and a citrus salad with a mint chiffonade, or try it with a grilled bratwurst and sauerkraut—if you like, try our sauerkraut recipe in chapter 10.

## INGREDIENTS

4 tablespoons butter

1 lb. potatoes, peeled, boiled, and mashed with milk and butter to your desired consistency (leaving it a bit chunky adds a nice texture and a satisfying bite to the dish)

3 leeks, sliced thin, rinsed, and drained (make sure to separate the rings to get the sandy grit out)

1 lb. curly kale (or Swiss chard) rinsed, stems removed and leaves roughly chopped

2 tablespoons EVOO

½ cup sour cream

½ cup bread crumbs

6 slices of bacon, cooked and crumbled

3 green onions, thinly sliced

Salt and pepper to taste

## MY METHOD

In a large, heavy-bottomed skillet over medium-low heat, melt 4 tablespoons of butter and add the leeks. Sauté until softened, 3–4 minutes. Add in kale and cook for 2 minutes, until slightly wilted. Remove from heat and scrape out onto a plate. Using the same pan, heat oil, add in potatoes and sour cream, and stir to combine. Sprinkle in bread crumbs and raise heat slightly. Allow the bottom to brown. Break up into pieces with a metal spatula, turning and scraping everything over to brown both sides. Continue to cook until most of the potato mixture is golden brown and has nice crisp bits. Return leeks and kale to pan and stir just until heated through. Remove from heat. Serve in a warm platter and garnish with the crumbled bacon and green onions.

# SUGAR

Question 18: Where did sugar cane originate?

Question 19: Who introduced sugar to Europe?

Question 20: What two plants are used to produce most sugar?

Question 21: What is the difference between white sugar and brown sugar?

Question 22: What country is the world's leading producer of sugar?

Question 23: What is bagasse?

Question 24: How do you make Vanilla Caramel and a Rustic Apple Tart?

Tracing a cultigen like sugar cane from its origin to its present distribution is one of the original contributions of cultural geography to the Body of Knowledge. Each domesticated plant (or animal) represented an important innovation, and as these new ideas spread, they were further changed—usually improved—with each step enabling a bit more in our survival epoch. We can argue about whether sugar is good for us, but we cannot dispute that sugar changed the world as much as any crop.

Most students trust their college professors, so the day I told my students that the word "vegan" was actually an Algonquin word that meant "poor hunter," most wrote it in their notebooks and probably expected it on an exam. At the time, vegan was just coming into common usage, but it is only one of a seemingly endless litany of food practices and traditions that are imbedded in human culture. For example, the Sepoy Mutiny in India was triggered in part by a new cartridge the British employed in the Enfield rifle. The ammunition was greased to permit easier loading. Hindus believed the grease was tallow (that is, beef fat), which was prohibited by Hindu belief, while Muslim troops believed the grease was lard, a pork product forbidden to Muslims.

Dr. G. says: The sepoys were native Indian troops in the employ of the British East India Company. Their mutiny, which shook the British Empire to its core, occurred in 1857.

Aside from religious beliefs and general food traditions, we have other voices in the food wars. The last I heard, the University of Hawaii had 700 students majoring in journalism. Adding in the rest of the potential reporters nationwide, we can expect a new food scandal in every Wednesday newspaper; political scandals can be manufactured for the front pages, but the food pages are probably more widely read and hence provide more jobs for writers. Mercury will be rediscovered in tuna fish, gluten will be found in flour, New York City will be banning trans-fat in their water supply, and toxic chemicals will be found to contain highly nutritious compounds. Two white crystals, however, will attract the most attention: sugar and salt. Strangely, neither are really foods (we add them to foods), and as far as I know, no religious groups ban them. I have carefully checked my supermarket shelves and found that the space devoted to salt and sugar substitutes is far greater than the space given to the real products.

The chemical definition of sugar encompasses a bunch of things, and the chemistry involved in refining and concentrating sugar is rather complex. Here, however, we are concerned only with the sugar that you may have in a bowl on your kitchen table (probably white stuff) or the brown variety that you may sprinkle over your

oatmeal. Sugar can be found in almost all plants, but it is sufficiently concentrated to be of use to us in only a very few. The most
common *is sugar cane, a grass that is probably native to New Guinea, or at least first
domesticated there.*

Sugar cane was also cultivated in Southeast Asia by 500 BC, and
it was widely grown in India as well. Indian sugar was mentioned in
ancient Chinese manuscripts. In the fourth century BC, *according
to some sources, Alexander the Great's army carried sugar cane back to Macedonia.*
Strangely, nothing much became of it for a long time. Arab traders
seem to have done better with it, and it began to be grown in the
Mediterranean area by the eighth century, almost exclusively in areas
controlled by Muslims.

The Portuguese and Spanish developed an extensive sugar industry in their Atlantic islands (Madeira, the Canaries, and the Azores),
then carried the crop to the New World. The Caribbean became the
center of the world sugar industry. The modern plantation system
may have begun with sugar. This agricultural system produces one
crop, requires extensive tracts of land, and lots of manual labor.
Workers' entire lives centered on the plantation.

Sugar cane and the plantation system were a main cause of colonization and slavery. The "sugar colonies" in the New World produced
enormous wealth for European owners and were primarily responsible for the extensive slave trade that brought millions of enslaved
Africans to the Americas.

*Sugar can also come from another plant, the sugar beet (beta vulgaris).* German scientists selectively bred beets in the eighteenth century, but
Napoleon put the sugar beet on the map. Sugar cane from the
Caribbean, especially from Haiti, had helped make France, under
Louis XIV, the richest and probably most powerful nation in the
world. During the Napoleonic Wars, however, the British Navy
blockaded France and, to make matters worse, Haiti had declared
its independence and defeated a large French army. France had
no sugar source. Napoleon mandated the growing of sugar beets
and had two refineries built in the Paris area. Today, France is the

*Sugar cane (photo by bbf)*

*Sugar beet*

*French sugar beet factory (photo published in the French magazine* L'Illustration, *13 May 1843 issue)*

world's largest producer of sugar beets, followed by the United States. Beets, however, account for only about 20 percent of world sugar production.

Sugar is disappearing from its former haunts in the Caribbean and Hawaii. Labor costs in these areas have proved prohibitive, while tourism has become the primary industry. *The world's largest sugar producer today is Brazil, followed by India.* A consortium of southern African countries is also producing significant amounts of sugar.

Brown sugar can be an intermediate product in the process of refining white sugar. The difficulty with this approach is that the molasses content cannot be controlled and the grain size of the sugar is somewhat large. *So the conventional approach to making brown sugar is to add molasses to fully refined white sugar—*the darker the sugar, the more molasses has been added.

A final note on cane sugar production: a major myth has developed that sugar cane fields are burned to rid the cultivated land of snakes. While this is a desirable outcome in Queensland and Africa (and probably other places), sugar cane fields are primarily burned to rid the cane stalks of the parts of the plant that do not contribute to sugar production; this can be as much as 20 percent of the cane's biomass. Burning the fields both improves the quality of the sugar and reduces the tonnage that has to be transported to the mill for refining. *Once the cane has been pressed and the juice removed, the waste product is called bagasse.* Bagasse is sometimes burned to produce electrical energy. Bagasse has also been converted to use as cattle feed and building material (and may someday be part of the vegan's diet).

# *From Geography...*

# *...to Gastronomy*

~

Food for Thought:

*"Good apple pies are a considerable part of our domestic happiness."*

—Jane Austen

~

## *Recipes for:*

Vanilla Caramel
Rustic Apple Tart

# VANILLA CARAMEL

*Makes about 1 cup*

## INGREDIENTS

I cup heavy cream
¼ vanilla bean
I cup sugar
¼ cup water
I tablespoon vanilla extract

## MY METHOD

Pour cream into a medium, heavy-bottomed saucepan.

Split and scrape the vanilla bean and place the scraped seeds and pod into the cream.

Heat the cream and vanilla over medium heat until bubbles begin to form around the edges, gently stirring to disperse the vanilla seeds. Turn off heat, but keep warm.

In another medium, heavy-bottomed saucepan, cook the sugar with the water over high heat until the sugar is dissolved, washing down the sides of the pan with a silicone pastry brush. Continue cooking until a light-honey color forms. This should take about 5 minutes. Be careful—it can turn dark quickly and make the caramel difficult to work with.

Remove from the heat and stand back a little from the stove while you carefully pour and stir in the scalded cream. Allow to cool for a minute and stir in the vanilla extract. Serve warm drizzled over ice cream, apple pie, or chocolate soufflé. Enjoy!

# RUSTIC APPLE TART

*Serves 8*

I love this way of making what I call a "free form" pie. I love it because it offers the freedom from the perfection of picture perfect pie, meaning that no matter how you fold the crust, in the end, it always looks beautiful and all your own.

Making pastry in humid Hawaii can pose many challenges, including keeping my ingredients cold enough. I like to cut up my butter and place the chunks on a small glass plate in the freezer until just before I use them. Likewise, I place my measured water in a glass measuring cup to keep them both icy cold

## INGREDIENTS

For the Crust:
- 1½ cup all-purpose flour
- 1 tablespoon sugar
- ½ teaspoon salt
- 1 stick, plus 2 tablespoons very cold, unsalted butter, cut into pieces
- ⅓ cup ice water

For the Filling:
- 4 Granny Smith (or tart apple of your choice)
- 3 tablespoons sugar
- 1 teaspoon cinnamon
- 2 tablespoons vanilla infused honey
- 2 tablespoons unsalted butter

## MY METHOD

Prepare the crust. Pulse together in the bowl of a food processor fitted with the blade the flour, sugar, salt, and butter for 5 pulses.

Remove top of processor and sprinkle ice water over mixture. Place top back on and process for 10–12 pulses until dough just begins to come together. There should be visible pieces of butter in it.

Unroll a 2-foot length of plastic wrap onto a work space. Dump out dough onto plastic wrap. Using the plastic, gather up the dough and press into a disk, wrapping the dough at the same time. Refrigerate for at least 20 minutes.

Make filling. Peel, halve, and core the apples and slice them crosswise ¼-inch-thick (or you can use an apple-peeler-corer-slicer to do all this for you!). Save the best slices for the very top of the tart (about ⅓ of the slices) and roughly chop the rest. Combine the cinnamon and sugar in another small bowl.

Lightly flour a work surface and line a baking sheet with parchment paper, or spray with vegetable spray. Unwrap the chilled dough, and place one side of dough on floured surface, leaving the plastic wrap on the top. I use this method to keep the dough from sticking onto my rolling pin. Roll out dough underneath the wrap into an approximate 12 × 14 inch rectangle (although you can do a circle, or how I do it, which is somewhat between a rectangle and a circle). Using a dough scraper or metal spatula, carefully peel dough off of work space. Place dough, dough side down, onto baking sheet and peel off plastic wrap.

Spread chopped apples over the dough to within one inch of the edge. Drizzle the vanilla honey over the chopped fruit. Arrange the remaining slices on the top, in slightly overlapping rows or concentric circles. Sprinkle vanilla cinnamon sugar evenly over the apples and dot with the butter. Fold up the edges of the dough over the apples to make a border.

Bake at 400°F for 45 minutes, or until the crust is nicely browned and crisp. Transfer pan to a rack and allow the tart to cool. Serve warm or at room temperature.

Special equipment: Food processor, rolling pin, plastic wrap, baking sheet

Prepare ahead: The dough for the crust can be made ahead and kept in an airtight container for 2 days in the refrigerator, or wrapped tightly in plastic and frozen for up to 2 months.

Tips: Chill cut butter and water in freezer until ready for use; Use plastic wrap to keep dough from sticking to your rolling pin; Heat the honey in a small pan to make drizzling easier (sometimes honey crystallizes and can be difficult to work with).

Serve with: Whipped vanilla cream, vanilla ice cream, drizzle with vanilla caramel sauce, and sprinkle with Maldon crystals.

# CACAO

Olfactory geography ("the geography of odors") is not commonly practiced or taught, but it has its role in our understanding of our surroundings. It was possible, for example to travel to my aunt's house from my home by following odors emitted along the way. Many were foul orders indeed; the worst was a facility that produced a gas of some sort, which it vented to the open air. Some were at least moderately pleasant: an Italian restaurant and a dairy. Some were strange: for some reason an obscure side road held a concentration of fried fish stands. On a broader perspective, some towns and cities can be found downwind without need of a map or GPS. In particular, Valdosta, Georgia, and Tyrone, Pennsylvania, with their pulp and paper industries, are easy to find.

My favorite landscape smells, however, are associated with my return to college in late summer. En route to Penn State, I leaned that the border between New Jersey and Pennsylvania, while not a particularly sharp divide, was nevertheless dramatic. The smell transitioned between New Jersey's petrochemical atmospheric cocktail and Pennsylvania's newly mowed hay. In my undergraduate days, I would drive alongside the Oswego River (actually part of the New York State Barge Canal System) and smell chocolate being made by Nestlé in Fulton, New York. Although I was never a big consumer of chocolate, its odor was certainly attractive. Linnaeus, who did all that original genus and species naming, must have thought so too since he named the plant *Theobroma*: "food of the gods."

Cacao, from which chocolate is made, *is native to Mesoamerica and, before European arrival, was grown in Mexico and Guatemala.* A beverage was made from the cacao, which, apparently, was quite bitter. Columbus, who was in search of spices, brought cacao back to Spain on his fourth voyage (which touched on the coast of central America) and the wealthy Spanish developed a taste for the beverage, but it was too rare (and hence too costly) and too bitter to become a popular item until many years later.

The Aztec civilization, which fell to Spanish conquest, was a voracious consumer of the chocolate beverage but never cultivated or otherwise grew it. The Aztecs lived in upland areas of Mexico (Mexico City is more than 7,000 feet above sea level), and cacao can be successfully grown only in the tropical lowlands. A lively trade in cacao flourished between the Aztecs and lowland tribes.

As Europeans developed better ways to produce chocolate from cacao, and especially to sweeten it with sugar, a

*Cacao*

huge market for chocolate began to emerge. Cacao poured into chocolate factories in Europe and the United States. The cacao came, increasingly, not from its native Central America but from Africa where it was planted as a cash crop. Today, *the Ivory Coast produces about one-third of the world's cacao*; 70 percent of all cacao is grown in West Africa. The demand for chocolate has continually grown in recent years: world production of cacao has more than doubled in the last thirty years.

There are three kinds of cacao: Forastero, Criollo, and Triniterio. Ninety-five percent of world production (and all of Africa's production) is Forastero. Criollo is said to produce the finest chocolate, but the plant is hard to grow because it is susceptible to disease; the leading producer is Venezuela. Triniterio is a hybrid of the other two varieties.

I am reasonably certain that *the oldest chocolate factory in the United States was the one whose output I could smell on the way to college: the Nestlé plant in Fulton, New York*. I have been unable to find the exact year that the plant started in Fulton, but it is known that they brought in workers from Switzerland. It became part of Nestlé (based in Switzerland), which today is the world's largest food company. Under its auspices, milk chocolate was invented by Daniel Peter. If memory serves, milk chocolate was the principal product of the Fulton plant. Many of the manufacturing facilities in Fulton—indeed, throughout the northeastern US "rust-belt"—were burdened with equipment that was old and outdated. The Fulton plant closed in 2003.

Dr. G. says: The plant was purchased by a company based in the Ivory Coast, which, as we know, is the world's largest producer of cacao. The enterprise soon went bankrupt.

*Hershey is the nation's—and almost certainly, the world's—largest producer of chocolate.* Milton Hershey began his manufacturing career as the owner of the Lancaster Caramel Company. It proved highly successful, but he sold the company and began to manufacture chocolate in 1903 in his hometown, now named Hershey, Pennsylvania.

> Dr. G. says: Milton Hershey is famous for explaining his sale of his caramel company by noting that caramels were a fad, while chocolate was a forever thing.

The signature product of Hershey was the Hershey "Kiss," invented in 1903 and as popular today as ever. A good trivia question (though not geographic) is: how many Hershey kisses are produced per day: 80 million!

Harry Reese went to work at a Hershey dairy farm, later worked at the factory, and, eventually, designed his own line of candies. He opened his factory right in Hershey and got a tremendous break in 1941 when the United States began sugar rationing. Reese concentrated his production on one product that used less sugar. That single item—the peanut butter cup—made Reese a huge success (and, according to children I polled by the millions, is the single most coveted item by Halloween trick or treaters). After Reese's death, Hershey acquired the Reese Company.

One final thought on Hershey's. My mother inherited a family recipe that may have originated at about the time that powdered cocoa was first produced. Although she disliked chocolate even more than I did, she translated the recipe from old measures ("use butter the size of an egg") to modern equivalents. The result was the best cake I have ever eaten. I have tinkered with the recipe myself and have eliminated the tendency of the cake to easily fracture. I recently tried Hershey's Dark Cocoa in the recipe and found it improved an already perfect cake in both appearance and taste.

# *From Geography . . .*

*Mazatlán, Mexico (photo by bbf)*

# *. . . to Gastronomy*

*Chocolate on display—La Boqueria, Barcelona, Spain (photo by bbf)*

~

Food for Thought:

*"Let's face it, a nice creamy chocolate cake
does a lot for a lot of people; It does for me."*

—Audrey Hepburn

~

## *Recipes for:*

Grammy's Cocoa Cake—A Cake for The Next Generation with Vanilla Bean Buttercream Frosting and Bittersweet Chocolate Drizzle

# GRAMMY'S COCOA CAKE– THE NEXT GENERATION

*with*

## Vanilla Bean Buttercream Frosting and Bittersweet Chocolate Drizzle

*Makes 2, 8–9 inch cake rounds*

We enjoy this cake with every birthday celebration in my family—and have ever since I was a little girl. Don't second guess the unsweetened chocolate—it is so absolutely perfect paired with the sweetness of the vanilla bean buttercream frosting. I have changed this recipe a little after finding that sometimes the cake cracked in the middle (too dry). I researched and found that my grandmother's recipe is similar to the famous Hershey's Chocolate Cake recipe, but different enough to see that both offered some interesting components; Grammy used butter, Hershey uses vegetable oil—I use EVOO. Grammy uses soured milk, they used plain—I opt for the sour version (must be my Russian roots loving all things sour). I (of course) use more vanilla than both of theirs, but that goes without mentioning. Another issue was that the cake would often stick to the bottom of the pan—so preparation is imperative and allowing the cake to cool completely before removing it is also a must. If you do not have a traditional birthday cake or have only used the boxed variety, I hope you will be inspired to create a new tradition and try this—you will never look back. One last note—it is even better if you make it a day ahead, frost it, and refrigerate it.

## INGREDIENTS

**Butter for greasing the pans**
**2 tablespoons flour for flouring the pans**
**2 cups sugar**
**1¾ cup flour**
**¾ cup cocoa**
**2 teaspoons baking powder**
**1 teaspoon salt**
**2 eggs**
**1 cup buttermilk or sour milk (I use whole milk soured with a tablespoon of apple cider vinegar)**
**½ cup best quality EVOO**
**1 tablespoon vanilla extract**
**1 cup boiling water**

## MY METHOD

Prepare your pans by cutting out parchment rounds. I place the pans over the parchment and, with a sharp paring knife, gently trace the circle and then either tear or cut the circle with shears. Butter your pans well, sides and bottom. Place the parchment in the pans and butter the parchment. Sprinkle in about a tablespoon of flour and, tapping the sides and bottom, shake the flour around to coat. I place my pans on baking sheets for the ease of putting it in the oven.

Combine sugar, flour, cocoa, baking powder, and salt in a large bowl. Add in eggs, sour milk, oil, and vanilla and beat for two minutes. Stir in the boiling water. The batter will be thin. Pour into prepared pans. Bake at 350°F for 25 minutes and turn the oven off. Keep in the oven for another 10 minutes. The cake is done when you press gently on the center and the cake springs back or when a toothpick comes out clean. Remove from oven and allow to cool on racks completely. To make removal from the pans even easier, I will refrigerate the cooled cakes in their pans for 30 minutes or so. Then, rap the pans or drop them sharply on your counter to dislodge them from the bottoms. They should come out easily now.

# VANILLA BEAN BUTTERCREAM FROSTING

*Makes enough for a 2-layer cake*

This is the buttercream frosting that I learned to make from my parents. It is simple—just 4 ingredients, but they can be tinkered with to adjust the consistency of it. If you want it thicker, add less milk. If you want it thinner, add a little more milk. I like the frosting a bit thicker for cupcakes, a little thinner for a whole cake so I don't drag the crumbs when I am frosting it. This frosting is sensitive to heat, so it is best to make room in your refrigerator unless you are going to eat it right away. You can mix this by hand, but a hand blender or stand mixer is best to make it quickly.

## INGREDIENTS

½ lb. butter, softened

I to I½ lbs. powdered sugar, sifted

¼ to ½ cup whole milk

½ vanilla bean, scraped of its seeds, reserving the pod for another use

## MY METHOD

In the bowl of your stand mixer, beat the butter with about ½ cup of the sugar. Continue adding sugar until you have mixed in about 2 cups. With the motor still running, add in a drizzle of milk. Scrape down the sides of the bowl as needed. Continue to add sugar and milk, testing the consistency until you have achieved your desired thickness. Add in the scraped vanilla seeds and mix until the seeds are distributed.

*Grammy's chocolate cake: The next generation (photo by bbf)*

# BITTERSWEET CHOCOLATE DRIZZLE

## INGREDIENTS:

**2 ounces unsweetened chocolate**
**2 tablespoons butter or coconut oil**

## MY METHOD

In a double boiler or glass microwavable bowl, heat the chocolate and butter stirring until perfectly smooth.

# ASSEMBLY

Place one cake round on a cake plate. With a butter knife or spatula, frost sides and top with a thin layer as a crumb coat. Add a second coat on just the top. Add on your next cake round—make sure the parchment paper has been removed from the bottom! Give this round a crumb coat. Then give the whole cake another coat of the frosting, using sweeping motions to create scallops or try wetting your knife lightly to make it very smooth. Allow to set for about 10 minutes and then, using a fork, drizzle the chocolate mixture over the top and allow it to run down the sides as well. Allow to set or, even better, refrigerate overnight to get a fudgy-moist cake.

# PLAIN VANILLA

Vanilla is an amazing spice, but writing about it is like walking through a mine field. Research reporting on vanilla is often contradictory, and the experience of growers is often different from the reported research in scientific journals. Why so much contradiction? In part, attempts have been made to grow vanilla in different environments; different results are inevitable, but because world production is relatively small, proper research has not been conducted under all conditions. Further, speculation (some bordering on absurdity) seems to have replaced factual reporting about vanilla. In turn, this may well be based on the fact that vanilla is valuable, so counterfeit vanilla is sold in great amounts. Most householders in the United States—and in other countries for that matter—have no idea about the quality of the product that they buy when they purchase "pure vanilla extract."

As the first chapter of this book points out, the Spanish and Portuguese explorers were obsessed with spices—they were not only very valuable in Europe, but also lightweight and therefore easy to transport. They were particularly interested in cloves, mace, cinnamon, and black pepper, which grew in South India, Ceylon, and the Spice Islands (the Moluccas) in the East Indies. They searched the whole New World (and elsewhere) for these products, but found them only in Asia. Some of these spices are still reasonably expensive today, but the Spanish had a complete monopoly on vanilla, now the world's second most valuable spice. *The Spanish today actually grow the most valuable spice: saffron.* Some say the Mancha version of saffron (Spanish, of course) is the world's finest. They also had a complete monopoly on chocolate—not a spice, but a flavor or food. So, while Spanish explorers were tromping about the New World searching for what wasn't there, greatly offending the natives in the process, they could have cornered the world market on saffron, vanilla, and chocolate.

*       *       *

Is vanilla a spice? Indeed yes; some say it's the perfect spice. In the presence of sugar or alcohol, it "marries" flavors. Chef T, whose recipes grace this book, serves vanilla lemonade at her restaurant that is the best I have ever tasted. It is not vanilla flavored, but rather lemonade in which the citrus flavor and the sugar have been harmonized. Because good vanilla is scarce and expensive, I think many uses of it as a spice have yet to be developed. I, for example, am experimenting with its use in certain adult beverages. Of course some of these are already "vanilla flavored," but my goal is to use vanilla as a spice, not a flavor.

*Vanilla is native to Mexico.* Its species is *planifloria*. Because most people have heard of vanilla beans—and have even seen and used them—they assume that vanilla is a variety of bean, presumably cultivated in a field. *In truth,* V. planifloria *is an orchid, the only edible orchid.* Vanilla orchids grow as a vine, often up the trunk of a tree, or staked in a lathe house or greenhouse.

*Vanilla orchid (photo by bbf)*

*Senior author with vanilla vines (photo by bbf)*

Now the bad news. Vanilla is sold widely in Mexico at every cruise ship port and at many border crossings. Don't buy it. Mexico does produce good quality vanilla, but the chances are very high you won't find it being sold by street vendors. Some of what is being sold is not even vanilla, but a product made from a seed that smells something like vanilla. If I believe the TV series, *Breaking Bad*, the Mexican illegal drug trade produces a higher quality product than much of the so-called vanilla sold there.

*Until about 1841, vanilla could only be grown in Mexico because it could only be pollinated by a native Mexican bee.* Apparently, French planters in the Indian Ocean islands discovered that the flowers could be hand pollinated. This is a delicate operation requiring skilled hands. The real problem, however, is that plants blossom for only a few hours. Pollination must occur at the right moment—and the pollination has to be limited. With vanilla beans selling at times at over $200 per pound, owners naturally would like to pollinate every blossom available, but if they do, the orchid can be overstressed and die. I have often wondered if Mexican-bee smuggling has ever been tried. It would certainly cut the labor costs.

\* \* \*

What about Tahitian vanilla? This is often promoted by restaurants in ice cream or other deserts, and it certainly sounds appealing. Actually, the vanilla grown in French Polynesia is a different species. It's apparently a hybrid of the original *planifloria*. Is it any good? University professors love to use Latin expressions since they are the height of pretension and students can't argue about them since they have no idea what they mean. Here the operative Latin expression about Tahitian vanilla is *de gustibus non est disputandum* (freely translated, it means "different strokes for different folks").

The world standard for vanilla is usually considered to be "Bourbon" vanilla, which is produced in Madagascar (and I think in the

Comoros and Mauritius as well). Their vanilla extract is widely available in the United States under different labels. I regret that I cannot recommend Bourbon vanilla beans as highly as the extract; they seem often to be sold after they have already been used to produce extract and thus have lost some of their flavor.

There is some doubt about what country is the world's largest producer of vanilla. During the twentieth century, Madagascar led in production. Most sources cite Indian Ocean storms as a cause for its fall from the dominance of the vanilla trade. My own thought is that there was a decline in Madagascar production about the time that Coke came out with its Edsel equivalent—the New Coke. Coca-Cola was, at one time, the largest buyer of sugar and, I suspect, of vanilla as well—could it be that the New Coke didn't use vanilla (or at least not as much)? Unless we can break into the vault in Atlanta where the Coke recipe is held, we can't be sure. Today, Madagascar has probably recovered its position as the world's top producer, but Indonesia is right behind.

\*  \*  \*

In front of the hotel my parents operated in the Adirondacks of New York, someone built and operated a frozen custard stand each summer. No one knew who he was or who owned the land on which he built the stand. He was the sole owner or employee. Early each morning he would bring a milk pail filled with a custard/soft ice cream mix for the machine that produced the frozen product. At the time, I could buy a Sealtest Ice Cream cone, one scoop, for a nickel. He charged an outrageous 25 cents for his product! Moreover, while competitors either swirled their custard as it went into the cone, or produced overarching clumps (like a Gaudi building in Barcelona), this guy just sort of crammed the custard in the cone: each cone he filled looked different. He sold out every day. When my friends and I could afford a quarter (not often!), we bought them. It was the best soft ice cream I ever tasted.

Years later, by sheer coincidence, I talked to someone who knew the secret of the 25 cent frozen custard. At the risk of giving away a million-dollar recipe, I report that the dairy that produced the milk and cream that went into the mix also made tapioca pudding. One day they ran out of vanilla extract to add to the mix, but instead added the heavily vanilla-infused liquid that collects at the top of cooked tapioca. Normally, they threw this liquid away since it detracted from the appearance of the pudding, but now they added it to the custard mixture. The vanilla, having first interacted with the tapioca now interacted with the milk and cream to produce a deep-toned vanilla flavor. I suspect what they did was illegal, but it sure was a marketing success!

# From Geography...

## ...to Gastronomy

~

Food for Thought:

*"Vanilla is not so plain . . . in fact, it's romantic."*

—Jim Reddekopp, owner, Hawaiian Vanilla Company

~

*Recipes for:*

Vanilla Extract
Vanilla Bean Flan
Frozen Vanilla Custard

# MAKING YOUR OWN VANILLA EXTRACT

Vanilla is one of those mysterious unknown ingredients that people were unaware of when we started selling our products at the Kapiolani Farmer's Market. We ended up having to educate almost every single person who came up to our booth back in the early 2000s. At that time, the internet was fairly new to mainstream America and most of the information that we acquired on vanilla was gained by traveling or seeking out people who actually grew the orchid. One of the first marketing brochures we wrote began with the question, "Did you know that vanilla comes from an orchid?" It would spark interest and many more questions, which is one of the reasons we now hold educational events on our farm. Sharing what you know with others is a good thing.

One of the things we do every day at our mill is teach others how to create their own homemade extract. It is wonderful to show people that they don't need to be afraid of "messing up" this recipe—there really isn't a wrong way to do this one! Be adventurous! Just select your alcohol, split your vanilla bean, and insert it into a bottle—make it a beautiful one, or an old one, or an old olive jar—it doesn't matter! Shake it up every now and then and you've got extract to use in your kitchen after a few months.

*Makes one 12-oz. bottle*

Takes about 6 months, so plan accordingly

## INGREDIENTS

**3 vanilla beans**

**12 oz. alcohol of your choice, I use rum for baking, whiskey for savory applications**

## MY METHOD

Split the vanilla beans lengthwise and scrape the seeds out using the back of your knife, so you don't scrape out the woody parts of the pod as well. Scrape the knife edge into the bottle you will be using and deposit the seeds by dragging your knife along the edge. They will be oily and cling to everything, so try not to get them on your fingers too much or else you will have little brown seeds on you all day. Add in the split vanilla pods as well.

Add in your alcohol of choice. Cover tightly and shake gently to disperse the seeds. Set in a cool cupboard away from direct sunlight. Within 24 hours you will have a vanilla flavored alcohol that can be added to a beverage. For cooking purposes, allow the vanilla to steep in the bottle for 6 months, shaking it gently every few days, or whenever you feel like it (nurture it—you are creating something). It will become cloudy and dark brown. Now it is ready to use for cooking and baking.

To keep your extract going indefinitely, when you have used ⅓ (4 oz.), replenish the alcohol. Depending on how much extract you use, add a new bean every year, as needed.

# FROZEN VANILLA CUSTARD

*Makes 1½ quarts*

## INGREDIENTS

2½ cups whole milk
½ teaspoon salt
²/₃ cup sugar
6 egg yolks
1 tablespoon vanilla extract
2 tablespoons tapioca flour
²/₃ cup heavy cream

## MY METHOD

In a medium heavy-bottomed saucepan, combine the milk and salt. Heat until scalded and set aside. Allow it to cool before adding to the egg mixture in next step.

Using an immersion blender with a whisk attachment or a stand mixer, blend the sugar, egg yolks, and tapioca flour until they are thick and smooth and fall from the beaters like ribbons. With the machine on low, gradually add the milk. Increase speed to medium and fully incorporate. Scrape the mixture back into the saucepan and cook over medium heat, stirring constantly and watching carefully to lower the heat if needed. Cook until the custard coats the back of the spoon heavily. Be careful not to overheat—this mixture can curdle. If it does, push through a fine mesh sieve to strain out large pieces.

Have a bowl set in an ice bath and scrape the custard into it. Stir to cool. Press a piece of parchment on the top of the custard and refrigerate until chilled through.

In a chilled bowl, beat the heavy cream until soft peaks form. Remove parchment from custard, scraping the custard from the parchment back into the same bowl with a spatula, and fold in the whipped cream.

Pour into your ice cream maker and freeze according to your machine's instructions.

# CLASSIC VANILLA BEAN FLAN
# WITH CARAMEL

*Makes 8 individual flan*

## INGREDIENTS

1½ cups sugar, divided

⅓ water

1½ cups whole milk

1 cup heavy cream

½ vanilla bean, scraped directly into heavy cream, reserving
    pod for another use

5 eggs, lightly beaten

½ teaspoon Kosher salt (or vanilla salt, if you have it)

## MY METHOD

Make Caramel:

In a small, heavy-bottomed pot over low heat, combine ¾ cup
sugar with ⅓ cup water. Increase heat, bringing the mixture to a fast
boil. Do not stir, but swirl pot occasionally. Use a silicone pastry
brush dipped in water to brush down sugar crystals. When caramel is
a golden amber, remove from heat. Make sure to watch carefully—it
will go quickly from a workable liquid to rock hard candy. Working
quickly, pour caramel into 8 custard cups, swirling each cup to coat
the sides and bottom.

Make Flan:

Preheat oven to 325°F. In each ramekin, on top of the caramel,
sprinkle a small amount of salt. In a medium, heavy-bottomed pot
over low heat, combine milk, cream, scraped vanilla seeds, and
remaining sugar and stir until sugar is dissolved. Turn heat to the
lowest setting. Add in whisked eggs slowly, stirring constantly. Add
salt and stir. Remove from heat. Strain through a fine mesh sieve

(there will be small pieces of egg that need to be removed) into custard cups.

Place cups into a baking pan. Fill a large pitcher (or kettle) of hot water and place it next to your oven. Place pan with custard cups in the oven and carefully pour the water into the pan so that it comes halfway up the exterior of the cups. Bake until they are no longer jiggly in the center, about 45 minutes. Carefully remove cups from water and let stand on a rack for 30 minutes. Serve warm or chill at least 4 hours.

To serve, use a butter knife to cut around the sides of each cup and carefully invert onto your serving plate, allowing the caramel to flow around the flan. Enjoy!

*Pouring hot caramel for vanilla bean flan*
*(photo by T. M. Reddekopp)*

# THE FRENCH IN AMERICA

*Question 37: The French and Indian War was part of what broader conflict?*

*Question 38: What was the first US National Park east of the Mississippi?*

*Question 39: From what is the word "Cajun" derived?*

*Question 40: Who discovered and claimed Louisiana for France?*

*Question 41: What was the remainder of the Louisiana Purchase named after Louisiana was admitted as a state?*

*Question 42: What is the only state that lacks counties?*

*Question 43: How do you make Beignets with Spiced-Chicory-Chocolate Dipping Sauce?*

French history has always confused me. Why would French engineers, for example, world-renowned for their bridge-building, so completely botch the Panama Canal? Why would the French military, led to disaster by Napoleon in Russia, rally to him and be defeated again at Waterloo? The fate of the French in the New World, where they had vast holdings in North America, only to see them vanish, is equally puzzling. Why did Montcalm, holding a probably unassailable position in Quebec City, march out to defeat on the Plains of Abraham? Despite my confusion, however, French culture has endured in North America and the quality of their cuisine reigns supreme.

Early cartographers, attempting to depict North America, labeled Virginia and England's first colony, Newfoundland. Everything in between was called "Acadia." As time went by, new names like

Dr. G. says: The original name assigned by Amerigo Vespucci was "Arcadia" but later versions of North American maps dropped the *r*. Ironically, it is not uncommon to hear Acadia National Park called "Arcadia."

"Plymouth" and "Massachusetts" were added to the maps and Acadia became restricted to what are today Canada's Maritime Provinces—and a bit more. The first European settlers in the area were French, according to some historians, and they came mostly from French cities. These early settlers became known as "Acadians" and they were distinct from the French who settled in New France (Quebec).

In 1710, the British conquered Acadia and required that the Acadians swear an oath of allegiance to the British crown. From the very beginning, the Acadians had established excellent relations with the Indians that lived in the area; the principal tribe (the Miqmaq) were hostile to the British. The Acadians felt that pledging allegiance to the British would turn the Indians against them. They refused to sign. Despite this refusal, the Acadians lived on their land without serious incident for about forty-five years.

*The Seven Years' War, probably the first true world war, was fought in North America as the French and Indian War.* The Acadians helped the French in Quebec, and the British decided the easiest way to eliminate this threat in the Maritime Provinces was to expel the Acadians from their land. Altogether, more than 11,000 Acadians were removed, many from Nova Scotia, most between the years 1755–1762.

*When the United States created its first national park east of the Mississippi, it originally called it "Mount Desert" but later changed the name to Acadia National Park.* The area in which the park is located was very much a part of the region known as "Acadia." Some of the displaced Acadians went to France, others to the British colonies to the south (now the United States), and some eventually returned to Acadia, especially to the current province of New Brunswick. The Spanish, who held Louisiana at the time, welcomed them, in part because the Acadians were strong Catholics (as, of course, were the Spanish).

*Over time, the Acadians living in Louisiana had their nationality shortened to "Cajun."* Cajun traditions, music, and food may have had dim origins in Maritime Canada, but it is more accurate to argue that today's Cajuns are part of, and contributors to, a broader Louisiana creole culture.

*       *       *

*Louisiana had earlier been claimed by France as the result of explorations by Rene-Robert Cavelier, Sieur de La Salle.* La Salle may have been the most important of the early explorers of North America. He was instrumental in establishing the fur trade in the Great Lakes region and later voyaged down the Ohio River to the Mississippi and claimed the entire drainage system of the Mississippi for France. This was an immense area, much of which was later acquired by the United States as the Louisiana Purchase.

Failure to find the source of the Mississippi (and some of its tributaries) made La Salle's claim somewhat vague, but La Salle's real problem was at the other end of the river. He returned to France and obtained four ships, filled them with 300 settlers, and set off with the idea of establishing a colony along the river, but he was unable to find the mouth of the Mississippi. His expedition was plagued by a shipwreck and a pirate attack. The survivors landed in Texas and went eastward on foot, still looking for the river. Eventually, the group mutinied and La Salle was killed, still a long way from the Mississippi.

Dr. G. says: Lake Itasca, Minnesota, is usually considered the source of the Mississippi, but it wasn't identified until 1820.

Dr. G. says: Because the claim staked by La Salle included the drainage of the river system, the area included also the Missouri River. President Jefferson therefore ordered the Lewis and Clarke expedition to find the headwaters, or source, of the Missouri. This task was immensely difficult and probably of little importance compared to the expedition's other findings and its trek down the Columbia River to the Pacific. While Lewis and Clarke thought they'd found the source of the Missouri, they almost certainly didn't. There's still a lot of controversy about the source, but I'm pretty sure it's somewhere in Montana.

Louisiana became a state in 1812. The remainder of the Louisiana Purchase then needed a new name; having a Louisiana "state" and a Louisiana "territory" made little sense. *So the huge expanse of land, extending all the way to Oregon, was renamed the Missouri Territory.* Eventually, the Missouri Territory was broken up into smaller territories and, finally, into the states that we recognize today.

*Louisiana is the only state that lacks counties but instead uses "parishes."* The parishes function exactly as counties. It is tempting (and probably correct) to attribute the use of parishes to the Catholicism of both the Spanish and French who once owned Louisiana. Still, one can look to the island of Barbados, a former British colony, and see that it also uses parishes as civil divisions.

*Mississippi River*

# *From Geography...*

# *...to Gastronomy*

~

Food for Thought:

*"To all men whose desire only is to be rich and to live a short life,
but a merry one, I have no hesitation in recommending New Orleans."*

—Henry Bradshaw Fearon

~

## *Recipes for:*

Beignets and Spiced-Chicory-Chocolate Dipping Sauce

# BEIGNETS WITH SPICED-CHICORY-CHOCOLATE DIPPING (OR SIPPING) SAUCE

New Orleans is steeped in tradition, and we are fortunate to have neighbors and friends, Paul and Stephanie Donoho, who lived there while attending Tulane. The culture is rich with wonderful food, and we have been the very willing recipients of their hospitality. They have made us gumbo and jambalaya, introduced us to the King Cake, and also served us beignets. Perfect for Sunday brunch, an afternoon treat, or dessert, they are best eaten right after they have cooled a bit.

*Makes about 2½ dozen beignets and 1 cup of dipping sauce*

## INGREDIENTS

I cup water
8 tablespoons butter, cut into pieces
2 tablespoons sugar
I teaspoon salt
I cup all-purpose flour
4 eggs
I tablespoon vanilla extract
EVOO or vegetable oil for frying
Powdered sugar for sprinkling

## MY METHOD

Bring water, butter, sugar, and salt to a rolling boil over high heat. Reduce heat to low and add all of the flour at once. Using a wooden spoon to stir constantly, cook the mixture to reduce the moisture and until it becomes shiny, about 3–4 minutes. Remove from heat and dump the mixture into a stand mixer bowl. Add the eggs, one at a time, beating until each is incorporated. Your mixture should have a ribbon-like texture.

Heat oil in a large, heavy-bottomed pot to 360°F. Drop the batter by tablespoons, 5–6 in each batch, and cook until deep golden, turning occasionally to cook each side. Remove with a wire skimmer or wooden spoon to a paper-towel-lined baking pan. You can keep them warm in a preheated oven while you fry the rest of the beignets.

If you don't use all the dough, place it in an airtight container and refrigerate for up to 3 days or freeze for up to 6 weeks.

Put the powdered sugar into a fine mesh sieve and sprinkle over warm beignets. Serve with Spiced Chicory Chocolate and enjoy!

# SPICED CHICORY CHOCOLATE

## INGREDIENTS

6 oz. 60% dark chocolate pieces
¾ cup heavy cream
½ teaspoon chicory powder (if you don't have chicory on
hand, use espresso powder or instant coffee mixed with a
teaspoon of boiling hot water)
1 teaspoon vanilla extract
¼ teaspoon cinnamon

## MY METHOD

In a small, heavy-bottomed pot over medium heat, bring cream to just before the boiling point. Add in the rest of the ingredients, turn off the heat and stir until all of the chocolate has melted. Pour into a communal dipping bowl, or espresso cups for individual dipping (or sipping!). Enjoy!

*Beignets (photo by bbf)*

# THE RUSSIANS COME
# TO AMERICA

.................................................................................

*Question 44: What Russian Tsar worked as a shipbuilder in Holland?*

*Question 45: What Dane traveled by land across Russia, built ships on the Pacific Coast, explored, then returned by the same route—and did it twice?*

*Question 46: What was the first capital of Russian Alaska?*

*Question 47: US Secretary of State William Seward negotiated the sale of Alaska by Russia to the United States; from what state was the US president at that time?*

*Question 48: In which decade did most Russians come to America?*

*Question 49: How do you make Russian Borscht?*

.................................................................................

Geographies of empire may be of two basic types: the Roman/British system and the American/Russian system. As the British and Roman empires developed, they did so largely by the addition of colonies. That these colonies were not considered part of the homeland was one of the fundamental causes of the American Revolution. The American and Russian empires, on the other hand, grew by accretion. The Americans expanded west; the Russians mostly east and south. Thomas Jefferson made the American system clear in the Northwest Ordinance and reaffirmed it in the Louisiana Purchase: we were not adding colonial additions (subservient to the United States) but expanding the size of the country.

Peter the Great of Russia earned the "Great" after his name for good reason. Russia became an empire during his reign. Peter westernized Russia, bringing about changes in customs, politics, and the economy. He expanded Russian territory to both the east and the west and had aspirations for a Russian navy even before Russia had a decent port. He traveled to Western Europe, where he learned about city construction in Manchester and naval operations in Malta. And, of course, he built the city of St. Petersburg. *The Tsar of Russia was possibly the most autocratic ruler in the world, yet Peter went to Holland and worked as a laborer in the shipyards.*

The seventeenth century, in which Peter the Great reigned, is often called the "Dutch century" because the Dutch so dominated trade with the East Indies and much of the fur trade in North America. The Russian economy was dependent on the fur trade at the time; Peter's trip to Holland and the knowledge he took back to Russia was invaluable.

*Church of the Savior on Spilled Blood, St. Petersburg, Russia (photo by bbf)*

Dr. G. says: At the time of Peter the Great's visit to Amsterdam, Holland had the world's greatest ship-building industry, greater even than Britain's. Among other technology that Peter took back with him was the fire hose, invented in Holland.

\* \* \*

Geographers are natural explorers because geography has a great interest in what is just over the horizon or around the next curve. Some people are motivated to become geographers by reading the exploits of famous explorers, many of whom were ship captains. These explorers/captains were portrayed as heroes, but at the same time, one of the great literary themes is the mad sea captain. Noah seems to have gone a bit balmy, Captain Ahab, while mildly reminiscent of a dean I knew, couldn't keep an even keel, and Captain Bligh seems to have become quite unchristian. Speculation has risen that the "madness" of ship captains may have arisen from the pewter plates often used aboard ship by captains. Pewter is mostly tin, but older pewter contained lead; newer pewter that might come in contact with the human body contains either no, or very little, lead. Lead poisoning can lead to dementia and death.

Dr. G. says: Personally, I was motivated to become a geographer by the money. I remember reading that the average geography graduate made more money than even a rocket scientist. It turned out basketball star Michael Jordan was a geography major at the University of North Carolina and jacked up the average substantially. So it hasn't worked out all that well for me—and it's now too late to perfect my jump shot.

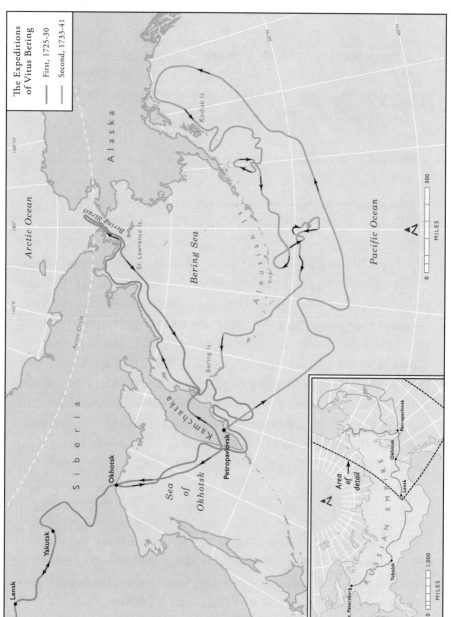

Vitus Bering's voyages

There is no evidence that Vitus Bering used pewter utensils—or was mad—but his voyages were the undertakings of a madman. He undertook incredibly long and arduous expeditions, which accomplished little and basically replicated the routes other Russian explorers had already taken.

Russian Tsar, Peter the Great, thought there was some small chance that Siberia was attached to North America and therefore sent *the Danish ship captain, Vitus Bering,* to find out. Bering went overland across Russia and Siberia to the Pacific. Once there, he built ships to explore the Arctic. He found out very little, and then returned overland to St. Petersburg. He set out shortly thereafter to repeat the trip. On his second voyage, he definitively proved that North America and Siberia were not connected. Captain Cook named the body of water separating the land masses after Bering—Bering Strait. Actually, the strait had been discovered ten years before Bering got there by another Russian explorer, Semyon Dezhnev. Generations of school kids are grateful for Cook's action (Semyon Dezhnev Strait is obviously a spelling and pronunciation demon).

The most famous town in Russian Alaska was Sitka. In the early part of the nineteenth century, it was the largest community on the west coast of North America. *It did become the capital of Russian Alaska, but not the first one. The original capital was Kodiak.*

\* \* \*

William Seward, whose name is firmly linked to Alaska, was one of the most notable statesmen of his era. He left the Whig Party to become a Republican and was favored to win the presidential nomination in 1860. When Lincoln got the nomination instead and was then elected president, he named Seward as his secretary of state. Despite all of Seward's accomplishments, today he seems remembered only for "Seward's Folly," the purchase of Alaska from Russia in 1867. It was hardly a folly then or now but was labeled as such by a few newspaper writers. *The US president at the time of the purchase of Alaska was not Lincoln, but Andrew Johnson,* the only Southern senator to remain loyal to the Union. Johnson was from Tennessee.

> Dr. G. says: Johnson was the only president to serve in the Senate after being president.

\*    \*    \*

Russians living in Alaska who stayed after the purchase by the United States became US citizens, but other Russians have been migrating to the United States in significant numbers since the end of the American Civil War in 1865. A startling statistic is that, in 2012, over 800,000 families in the United States spoke Russian as their "at home" language.

Answering the question posed at the beginning of this chapter leads to major problems of definition. Millions of people FROM the Russian Empire came to the United States, but not all were considered by US immigration authorities to BE Russian. Probably the largest group in the "from Russia, but not Russian" group were Jews. The home language of many of the Jews was Yiddish. *It appears that most "from Russia" immigrants came in the decade 1901–1910. There are other immigration figures, however, that show the number of immigrants who spoke Russian as a first language peaked in the decade 1911–1920. Take credit for either decade.*

# *From Geography . . .*

# *. . . to Gastronomy*

~

### Food for Thought:

*"A glass for the vodka, for the beer a mug, and for the table, cheerful company."*

—Russian Proverb

~

## *Recipe for:*

Russian Borscht

# RUSSIAN BORSCHT

*Serves 10–12*

I love the whole idea of this recipe; the bright color, the subtle sourness of apple cider vinegar, the small pieces of vegetables, dill, sour cream—it all just melds into such a warm, soul-filling dish. Don't let the amount of ingredients fool you into thinking this is difficult! A food processor makes the fine chopping a quick job. You can choose to make this as chunky or smooth as you want it—follow the optional instructions if you prefer a smoother consistency—but take note that it will not be a truly creamy soup, just not as chunky. Perfect with a cool cucumber salad, a large, crusty loaf of whole grain or Russian rye bread, and good salted butter. *Prijatnovo appetita!*

## INGREDIENTS

3 tablespoons EVOO

2 medium beets, peeled and chopped fine in food processor

1 medium carrot, peeled and chopped fine in food processor

1 onion, peeled and chopped in food processor

2 celery ribs, chopped in food processor

1 14 oz can chopped tomatoes

5 medium russet potatoes (about 3 lbs.), peeled and chopped in food processor

½ to ¾ medium cabbage, chopped in food processor (about 5 cups)

¼ cup apple cider vinegar

3 garlic cloves, thinly sliced

3 bay leaves

½ tablespoon dried dill weed

3 quarts vegetable or beef stock or water (if you have bone broth, this is a perfect recipe to use it—use 2½ quarts of stock and 2 cups of bone broth)

Salt and pepper to taste

**Serve with:**
**Fresh, chopped dill weed**
**Sour cream**

## MY METHOD

In a large heavy-bottomed stock pot, heat oil over medium-high heat.

Add in beets, carrot, onion, celery, tomato, potatoes, and cabbage. Cook, stirring occasionally for about 10–15 minutes or until the vegetables are beginning to brown a bit and soften.

Turn up heat and continue cooking for another minute. Add in the cider vinegar and stir constantly for one minute.

Add in garlic, bay leaves, and dill weed. Cook for another minute, stirring.

Add stock or water and bring to a boil. Reduce heat to medium low and simmer for 20–30 minutes, or until vegetables are tender. Remove bay leaves. A completely optional next step: With an immersion blender or in batches in a blender, blend about half of the soup, leaving the rest in small chunks. This is up to you if you prefer a smoother consistency for your borscht. You can choose to leave it "as is" as well.

Serve with salt and pepper, fresh dill, and dollops of sour cream.

*Borscht ("Borscht Served" by Liz West from Boxborough, MA)*

# JEWS IN AMERICA

Question 50: Where did Sephardic Jews originate?

Question 51: Where was the first Jewish congregation in (what is now) the United States?

Question 52: In 1795, what US city had the greatest concentration of Jews?

Question 53: Where was the first Ashkenazi congregation in the United States?

Question 54: What was the principal language of Sephardic Jews—and of Ashkenazic Jews?

Question 55: What country today has the greatest number of Jews?

Question 56: How do you make Challah?

I was actually there when the first bagels were offered at the campus center dining room at the University of Hawaii. At the end of the cashier's line was a bagel salesman, giving anyone a free bagel. Every student politely refused, saying, "I don't eat bagels." Within a year, bagels were one of the most popular breakfast items at the same dining room. The amazing part of this transition was that the bagels being given away and sold at the campus center were not very good. Bagels are, of course, the quintessential Jewish contribution to the American diet.

Are Jews a racial, ethnic, or religious group? Depending on when and where you ask this question, you'll get different answers. Anthropologists have convincingly argued that race is a myth—that physical differences among groups of people are too slight to constitute "races." Even when people firmly believed in races, however, it was impossible to consider Jews to be a race simply because we can find African Jews, Indian Jews, Chinese Jews—and this is only a partial list. In the United States, we can argue that Jews have become more religious over time because synagogue memberships have gone up. On the other hand, there is some evidence that Israeli Jews have become more secular. It is a tough question, and like all university professors, I can skip over it and suggest YOU think about it (and it will be on the next exam).

Dr. G. says: Ladino is Judeo-Spanish. The grammar and some of the vocabulary come from older versions of Spanish. It is still spoken in Israel and parts of the Middle East and Asia Minor where the Sephardi moved.

There are two main groups of Jews in the world: Sephardi and Ashkenazi. *The Sephardi are Spanish Jews by the very meaning of the word,* and their history is fascinating. By 1492, Jews had developed a distinctive culture in the Iberian Peninsula. In that year, however, the Spanish Jews were given three choices: 1) convert to Christianity; 2) leave Spain; or 3) be executed. The Spanish assumed that most would convert; however, many left. *They carried their language, Ladino, with them.* In some areas where the Sephardi relocated—in areas conquered by Islamic Arabs—the preexisting Jews adopted Sephardic religious practices. At the same time, most Sephardi gave up Ladino and began to use Arabic.

Some Sephardi also relocated to the Netherlands and to England. *They were the first Jews to come to the colonial United States, establishing the first two American synagogues in New York City and Newport, Rhode Island.* Any synagogue in the colonial United States was a Sephardic house of prayer. *The largest concentration of Jews in colonial America may be a surprise to you: it was in Charleston, South Carolina!*

\* \* \*

The larger group of Jews in Europe (and certainly in America) was well established by 1000 AD in Central Europe. *The Ashkenazi, like the Sephardi, also had a distinctive language: Yiddish,* a mostly German dialect with Slavic and Hebrew (or Aramaic) overtones. The Ashkenazi found themselves as outsiders in a tight-knit feudal system in Europe. Occupations that they could follow were extremely limited and persecution by the surrounding Christian community was severe.

In the late 1700s, Catherine the Great of Russia designated an area (then under Russian control) where Jews were allowed to settle. Called the "Pale of Settlement," it included parts of present day Poland, Lithuania, and the Ukraine. By the beginning of the twentieth century, with 5 million Ashkenazi, it contained (probably) a majority of the world's Jews—and a lot of the poorest.

*The first Ashkenazic synagogue in the United States was built in Philadelphia in 1795.* Significant numbers of Ashkenazi, however, did not arrive in the United States until the 1840s when a migration of relatively well-off Jews migrated from Germany.

By 1880, two processes affecting the Ashkenazi were well underway. First, in western Europe, Jews had attained a significant measure of assimilation; for example, a Jew (Disraeli), had become prime minister of the United Kingdom. Still, there were some disquieting moments, such as the Dreyfus case in France in which an innocent French army officer, who was Jewish, was convicted of treason. Second, millions of Jews living in the Pale of Settlement had begun to move out. Millions came to the United States between 1880 and 1920, both from the Pale and from other areas of Eastern Europe. For the most part, they were poverty stricken and settled overwhelmingly in the New York City area.

\* \* \*

"The Holocaust" was a term I had never heard used until long after the event, and the facts surrounding it unfolded over several decades of my life. The hundreds of books, movies, TV programs, and articles that emerged had an incredible emotional impact on not only me, but, of course, on millions of others. It was not, however, until scholars began to write their unemotional accounts of the Holocaust that the real horror of the events overwhelmed me. Previous persecutions of Jews over the centuries had held out the possibility that conversion to Christianity would be a saving option, but in Hitler's Germany even Christians who had but a single Jewish grandparent were subject to execution.

Some sources say that the Holocaust began with the German invasion of the USSR in 1941 and the subsequent murder of the Jews living in the remnants of the Pale of Settlement. Voices seeking the elimination of Jews, however, were raised in Germany in the 1890s and certainly Hitler had espoused it in the 1920s. American Jews were safe from the Holocaust because of America's location and military power—not because Hitler decided to overlook them. Indeed, the Nazis had developed specific plans to eliminate Jews even in countries their armies never reached.

Dr. G. says: US censuses in the early twentieth century listed race based on the census enumerator's opinion. "Jewish" was commonly listed, but it seems to have been indiscriminately applied to many immigrants from Eastern Europe.

The death of an estimated six million Jews during the Holocaust meant that the United States contained a majority of all Jews by 1945. *Today, the Jewish populations of the United States and Israel are roughly the same.* The US Census does not permit questions about religious preference, so we cannot be sure about the number of Jews in the United States; however, we can be sure that the number of Jews in Reform (or liberal congregations) has declined due to low birth rates, whereas those in Orthodox congregations have increased in number due to higher birth rates.

# *From Geography . . .*

## *. . . to Gastronomy*

~

Food for Thought:

*"There are people in the world so hungry, that God
cannot appear to them except in the form of bread."*

—Mahatma Gandhi

~

## *Recipe for:*

Challah

# CHALLAH

*Makes 2 lovely braided loaves*

For some reason, I love to make Challah. In fact, I make a similar recipe for our Vanilla Sweet Buns that we serve to all of our guests at our vanilla mill. It is always interesting that I choose to make it, almost as a calming agent, when we are having a big dinner or event. I will make a huge batch of it and set it to rise in every bowl I have in my kitchen. My husband and my children will shake their heads in dismay—but making this beautiful bread always seems to calm me.

## INGREDIENTS

2 cups milk, warmed slightly

½ cup sugar

½ cup room temperature butter, cut into 1 inch pats

7 cups all-purpose flour, divided (just measure out all of your flour into a bowl—you will need ½ cup measured from this for the starter)

1½ tablespoons dry yeast (or 2, ¼ oz. packages)

½ cup warm water

1 tablespoon kosher salt

2 eggs, beaten, plus one egg for brushing loaf

## MY METHOD

In a medium saucepan over medium heat bring the milk to a light simmer (you will see bubbles forming around the edge of the pan). Once bubbles form, continue heating for 30 seconds and then remove from heat onto a cooling rack. Add in sugar and stir until the sugar has dissolved. Then add in butter and allow it to melt. Stir to assist with the cooling and set aside.

In a large glass measuring cup or bowl, add ½ cup of flour. Add in yeast and salt. Stir to combine and add in warm water. Stir again and allow the yeast to work. Let it rest for 5 minutes in a warm spot in the kitchen. You should see bubbles forming to indicate that the yeast is alive. If there are no bubbles, you may have inactive (or dead) yeast and will have to start over with fresher yeast.

Once you are sure the yeast is active, add in two eggs and scrape this mixture into the bowl of your stand mixer and attach your dough hook. If you will be hand stirring, use a big bowl and a good long-handled wooden spoon. I find that a stainless steel bowl is the best because it is light enough to hold in one hand, bowl tucked into the crook of one arm, stirring with the other.

Add the cooled milk-sugar-butter mixture into your mixing bowl then add in half of your remaining flour and gently mix to somewhat incorporate the flour—do this at the lowest setting or just by hand so that the flour does not come flying out at you from your mixer. With the machine running, slowly sprinkle in the rest of the flour and then continue to mix until the dough comes together (it should be very thick—if you have to stop your machine to pull the dough off the hook to knead better, please do so). When the dough pulls away from the sides of the bowl, turn the machine off and dump out dough onto a lightly floured surface.

Lightly dust your hands with flour and knead the dough until it is smooth, pliable, and springs back when lightly pressed. This should take 8–10 minutes. Use no more flour than is absolutely necessary.

Oil the bottom and sides of two bowls. Divide the dough into halves with a bench scraper or sharp knife and place each portion into a bowl. Cover with a flour sack towel and place in a warm place to rise for two hours, punching the dough down every 20–30 minutes. The more you punch down the dough, the better the flavor of the bread, but allow it to rise again before punching it down—in 20–30 minute increments.

During this rising time, prepare your baking sheets. It is best to use one for each of the loaves. Line them both with parchment and give them a light spray or brush of oil.

When the 2 hours are up, punch down one last time and dump the dough rounds onto your counter. Using a bench scraper or knife, divide each round into three mostly equal parts (they don't have to be exact). Using your hands, using rolling and gently pulling motions roll into a strand about 12 inches long. If the dough resists, allow it to rest for a few minutes and try again. The gluten may need to relax a bit. Repeat with the remaining portions.

Braid 3 strands together to form a simple braid, tucking and pressing the edges gently to turn under. Carefully lift the dough and place onto the prepared baking sheets. Repeat for remaining loaf. Place loaves in a warm place and allow them to rise for 30 minutes or until plump and almost twice the size of what you started with.

Preheat oven to 375°F.

Beat the remaining egg and brush the loaves all over, making sure to get down the sides and into the crevices. You can now sprinkle with sesame seeds or poppy seeds, but I never do. They are so beautiful when they come out of the oven 30 minutes later, perfectly golden brown. So make your choice and go ahead and bake them for 20 minutes. Then turn your oven off and allow them to finish cooking as the heat slowly reduces. Pull them out after another 10 minutes. Cool on racks.

Eat right away or give them away with whipped honey butter or save it for tomorrow's French toast or wrap it and freeze it for your Thanksgiving supper or make an incredible bread pudding with it—enjoy!

Challah (photo by T. M. Reddekopp)

# IMMIGRANTS, PART I

.....................................................................................

*Question 57: What is the official language of the United States and what almost became its official language shortly after independence?*

*Question 58: What ancestry is claimed by the largest number of Americans?*

*Question 59: What was the largest immigrant group to fight in the Union Army during the Civil War?*

*Question 60: Who was the American Ace of Aces in WWI?*

*Question 61: What New York Yankee provided jars of pickled eels to his teammates?*

*Question 62: From what immigrant group were John D. Rockefeller, John Jacob Astor, and Donald Trump descended?*

*Question 63: In what river was the battleship* Graf Spee *scuttled?*

*Question 64: How do you make Mom's Sauerkraut and Apples?*

.....................................................................................

From time to time, I find it necessary to debunk pseudo-trivia. Some false trivia appears in TV game shows, cruise ship trivia games, and even on news networks. One question that I have heard repeatedly asked concerns a language that "almost" became the official language of the United States. In the first place, there is no official US language. At various times, and for various reasons, US states have felt compelled to declare an official language; at last count, thirty-one states have such a law. Moreover, laws restricting the use of non-English languages on the telephone, over short-wave radio, and even on train station platforms have been enacted. *One pervasive myth, however, is that German almost became the official language of the country. When I first heard this on a TV show, I attempted to confirm it. I couldn't (although I encountered a lot of people who thought it was so). I still can't.*

\* \* \*

When the results of the 1990 census were released, more than 50 million Americans were said to be of German ancestry, outnumbering all other groups. In the 2000 and 2010 censuses, people were allowed to self-identify (previously, census-takers made the decision) and the number claiming German ancestry dropped significantly—but *German background was still the most common heritage of Americans.*

\* \* \*

Germans came to America in significant numbers for the first four centuries of settlement in what is now the United States. Most came during the nineteenth century and formed a significant portion of the population in a band extending from Ohio and Wisconsin through Missouri and into Texas. In some communities, German was not only the common language spoken, but also the language of instruction in the public schools. It is a pervasive myth that the Irish were *the most numerous immigrant group to serve in the Union army during the Civil War; in fact, it was the Germans.* Abraham Lincoln's campaign for the presidency in 1860 took particular care to woo German Americans (who had generally been members of the Whig Party) to become Republicans.

\* \* \*

German Americans seemed to largely avoid the waves of anti-immigrant sentiment that swept the United States in the nineteenth century, but that was to change considerably by the time of World War I. Anti-German sentiment began to rise in the United States even before the country entered the war. Stories of German atrocities in Belgium and France, some false, many exaggerated, were pervasive in the American press, which received news of the war only after it had filtered through Great Britain's propaganda apparatus. Businesses with German names in the United States sometimes changed their names, and sauerkraut became "liberty cabbage."

Dr. G. says: In Hawaii, Hackfeld's stores changed their name to Liberty House, which eventually became the largest department store chain in the territory and state.

While anti-German sentiment continued to simmer in the United States during WWI, the air war being fought by primitive airplanes over France featured at least one American hero of German ancestry that helped change people's thinking. The "bad guy," of course, was the Red Baron—Baron Von Richthofen—immortalized by Charles Shultz's Snoopy in the "Peanuts" comic strip. The "good guy," and *America's Ace of Aces, was Eddie Rickenbacker.* The Red Baron, apparently, was shot down by the ground fire of a Canadian soldier and killed.

Perhaps the two greatest baseball players to be teammates were Babe Ruth and Lou Gehrig; both were of German descent. In Gehrig's case, his mother and father were immigrants, struggling in the melting pot of New York City. *Gehrig's mother pickled eels caught in the East River, and Lou would share jars of them with other members of the New York Yankees.*

*         *         *

German Americans also achieved considerable wealth and prominence in the United States. *John Jacob Astor*

*Eddie Rickenbacker*

*Lou Gehrig*

*was one of America's earliest tycoons and achieved his wealth in the fur trading busi-*
*ness. Later, John D. Rockefeller may have become the richest man in all history through*
*his dominance in the oil refining business. The Rockefeller family, through its trusts and*
*foundations, still makes its influence felt today. TV star and politician, Donald Trump,*
*claims German ancestry.*

Although the village in which I spent my early life had once been
known as "Little Ireland," by the twentieth century it had become in-
habited by large numbers of German immigrants. When WWII broke
out, a surprising number of people living in the village who were
thought to be Germans turned out to be Austrians—until it was determined that Adolf Hitler was born in Austria. At that point, a number

of the older people claimed to be Dutch! The second and third generation Germans in my community, however, were perfectly content to acknowledge their German ancestry, even as they enlisted in the armed forces. This was happening throughout the United States, and it was no coincidence that someone with the German name "Eisenhower" became the commander of allied troops in Europe!

From the standpoint of Great Britain (and Winston Churchill, in particular), the decisive battle of WWII was the Battle of the Atlantic. If Germany could interdict Allied shipping in the Atlantic, Britain could not have survived, armaments sent to the Soviet Union would not have made it there, and there could have been no D-Day invasion. German submarines in the Atlantic were a fearsome weapon, but if the Germans had been able to add surface ships to their U-boat fleet, the outcome of the war might have been entirely different. In fact, Nazi Germany succeeded in getting two battleships into the Atlantic at the beginning of the European phase of WWII. The more famous of the two, the *Bismarck*, was sunk by the British Navy after the *Bismarck*'s steering system had been damaged beyond repair. The other ship, the *Graf Spee*, was trapped in the South Atlantic by the British and took shelter in Montevideo, Uruguay. Under the rules of neutrality (Uruguay was a neutral nation), the *Graf Spee* *could stay in Montevideo for only a limited time. Eventually, she left port, apparently to confront the British who waited for her in the Rio de la Plata (and the Atlantic), but her captain scuttled her at the mouth of the river.*

Dr. G. says: Under the rules of WWI disarmament, Germany was not allowed to build battleships, but by clever design and material innovation, the Germans were able to build ships within the guidelines that were more than a match for British battleships.

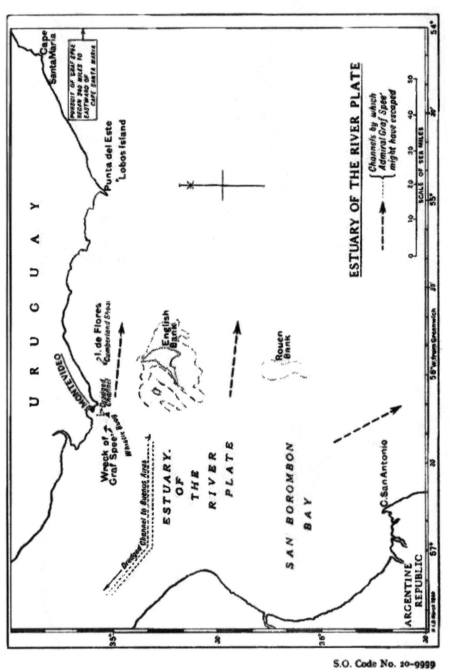

Site of the scuttling of the Graf Spee—Rio de la Plata, Uruguay

# From Geography . . .

*Statue of Liberty (photo by bbf)*

# . . . to Gastronomy

*Sauerkraut (liberty cabbage) (photo by bbf)*

~

Food for Thought:

*"Those who do not eat well on Christmas Eve will be haunted by demons during the night."*

—German tradition

~


***Recipe for:***

Mom's Sauerkraut and Apples

# MOM'S SAUERKRAUT AND APPLES

Ah, another sour (or sauer) recipe! This goes so well with roasted and braised meats, bratwurst, and polish dogs. The apples add sweetness to the sour, and the potatoes lend creaminess to the contrasting crunch of cabbage.

## INGREDIENTS

2 tablespoons butter

1 small onion, thinly sliced

3 apples, peeled, cored, and thinly sliced

2 cups prepared sauerkraut, rinsed and drained

¼ cup water

½ teaspoon salt

1 tablespoon sugar

½ teaspoon caraway seeds

2 small potatoes, peeled and grated

## MY METHOD

In a medium saucepan, melt butter on medium-low heat. Add onion and apples and cook until softened but not browned, about 10 minutes.

Add in remaining ingredients and cook for 10 minutes.

# IMMIGRANTS, PART II

*Question 65: Where is the Mezzogiorno?*

*Question 66: What is the tallest mountain in Italy?*

*Question 67: What is the highest volcano in Italy?*

*Question 68: What Republican mayor of New York had a Jewish mother (Irene Coen), was an Episcopalian, and went to high school in Prescott, Arizona?*

*Question 69: In what American city was Al Capone born?*

*Question 70: Who was born in Martinez, California, wore the number 5 in his athletic career, and was nicknamed for a Pan American airliner?*

*Question 71: How do you make Cannoli Bites with Dark Chocolate?*

I began the study of geography at Penn State full of trepidation and ignorance. At one of the initial meetings of new graduate students, a professor spoke despairingly of people not knowing the difference "between a caldera and a drumlin." I was one of them. Almost as bad, the head of the department was a well-known expert on the Soviet Union who had switched his area of interest to the Mezzogiorno; I had no idea where or what that was. Within the context of his remarks, I discovered that it had something to do with Italy, but I could not find the term in my atlas, dictionary, or encyclopedia, and I was fearful of betraying even more ignorance by asking anyone that might know. My godparents had been born in Italy, so I asked them. They'd never heard of the term and thought some-

*Italy in Roman times*

one was pulling my leg since it literally means "middle of the day." Eventually, I learned that *Mezzogiorno refers to southern Italy, both the main-land portions and Sicily.* It is important to the United States because most Italians who migrated to the United States came from the Mezzogiorno, a generally rural and impoverished area of Italy at the time of the migration.

> Dr. G. says: A caldera is the really big collapse of land, generally ring shaped, that follows a volcanic eruption (Yellowstone National Park is mostly a caldera), while a drumlin is a hill that results from a melting glacier's deposition of materials it carried. Geologists reading this may quibble with my definition, but I am grateful I've gotten this close!

\* \* \*

Really good trivia questions are those that seem easy, but trip up even expert players. When asked about the tallest mountain in Italy, *the trivia expert will immediately think of volcanoes, of which Italy has a number. By far the tallest of these is Mt. Etna, on the island of Sicily.* This location will validate this answer (in the trivia master's mind) since an offshore location seems slightly obscure and hence more likely to be correct. In fact, *the tallest mountain in Italy is also the tallest mountain in France: Mont Blanc*—or Monto Blanco if you prefer. The mountain lies right on the border between the two countries.

\* \* \*

The area just south of Mt. Blanc is the area the Romans (in Julius Caesar's time) called "Cisalpine Gaul," the area of Gaul on this side (the Roman side) of the Alps. It only became Gaul around

400 BC when the Gauls came through the Alps from the northwest. The Romans didn't care for this, but suffered defeat after defeat in Cisalpine Gaul from the Gauls directly or from the Gauls allied with the Carthaginians. The ability of the Romans to gain control of this region—especially the valley of the Po River—goes a long way to explaining the success of the Roman Empire. Initially, Cisalpine Gaul was a province of Rome, then it became a part of Rome itself. One of its borders was the legendary Rubicon River; "legendary" is the correct term because today no one is sure exactly where the river was—or even whether it still exists today.

Italians came to the United States long before the United States was a country and certainly long before Italy was a country. Nevertheless, most Italians migrated to the US between 1880 and 1920; during those four decades Italy sent more migrants to the US than any other country. The vast majority was from the Mezzogiorno and, generally, from rural areas. At the time of their arrival, however, the American frontier, with its promise of free land in the West, was closed. Italians mostly settled in the cities of the eastern United States.

*One of the most unusual politicians in US history emerged as the son of Italian immigrants. Fiorello La Guardia was born in Greenwich Village in New York City. His father was born in Italy; his mother (Irene Coen) was Jewish from Trieste (then part of the Austro-Hungarian Empire).* La Guardia spoke both Italian and Yiddish and attended high school in Prescott, Arizona, where his father played in the US Army band. After serving in the US state department and the US Congress, and earning his law degree, La Guardia, a Republican, became mayor of New York City. He established a close relationship with the Roosevelt New Deal administration and was able to get federal money for reinvigorating New York City. The many changes he brought about, especially improvements to Central Park, endeared him to both Republicans and Democrats. La Guardia is considered one of the greatest mayors in US history.

\* \* \*

Despite the noble accomplishments of multitudes of Italian-Americans, the association of crime bosses and Italians became fixed in the American mind. Mario Puzo's book, *The Godfather*, and the movies that followed from it sealed an idea that may have begun with Italian American Al Capone. Capone led the Outfit in Chicago, an organization that thrived on the illegal alcohol trade during Prohibition days. Capone was somewhat of a hero in Chicago—until the gang killings known as the Saint Valentine's Day Massacre swayed public opinion against him. Capone eventually was sent to prison for (of all things) tax evasion. *Many thought Capone was a native of Chicago, but he was really born in Brooklyn, New York, and moved to Chicago when he was in his twenties*—job openings in crime were better in Chicago!

\* \* \*

Not all Italian immigrants stayed in the big cities of the east and Midwest. One moved to Martinez, California, and later to San Francisco to engage in commercial fishing. He sired nine children, the eighth of which was named Giuseppe Paolo. Giuseppe hated fishing boats and was considered a lazy lout by his father, but was lucky enough to get a job playing shortstop on a baseball team due to a recommendation by his older brother. Giuseppe, later *Joe DiMaggio, became one of the greatest players in the history of the game. In his thirteen seasons with the New York Yankees, the Yankees won ten pennants, and Joe was an All-Star every year he played. His speed in center field was so great that he was called the "Yankee Clipper," after the Pan-American Clipper airplane.* His number 5 was retired by the Yankees.

*From Geography . . .*

*. . . to Gastronomy*

∽

Food for Thought:

*"After a good dinner one can forgive anybody, even one's own relations."*

—Oscar Wilde

∽

**Recipe for:**

Cannoli Bites with Dark Chocolate
The Godfather Cocktail

# CANNOLI BITES WITH DARK CHOCOLATE

*Makes lots of little dessert bites, perfect for a large gathering*

When the actor Richard Castellano (playing the role of Clemenza) in *The Godfather* tells his mob coworker to whack Paulie in the parked car scene, he said, "Leave the gun—take the cannoli"—which apparently was a completely improvised line. These little bites, comprised of all truly authentic cannoli—just deconstructed and improvised—can allow everyone to take the cannoli. Makes an elegant dessert for a themed dinner party or for a large crowd.

## INGREDIENTS

For the Filling:

2¾ cups fresh plain or vanilla ricotta (recipe found in chapter 24); drain the ricotta in a cheesecloth lined sieve if it is too wet—it should be dry

½ cup powdered sugar

3 tablespoons dark chocolate (I use Ghirardelli's 60%), shaved or chopped fine

I teaspoon vanilla extract

½ teaspoon orange zest

## MY METHOD

With a stand or handheld mixer, whip ricotta and sugar until fluffy. Fold in chocolate, vanilla, and orange zest. Cover and refrigerate.

## INGREDIENTS

For the Shells:

**2 cups flour**

**3 tablespoons sugar**

**1 tablespoon cocoa powder**

**1 teaspoon cinnamon**

**½ teaspoon salt**

**¾ cup sweet Marsala wine or sherry**

**¼ cup best quality EVOO**

**Oil for frying the shells**

**For serving:**

**Chopped dark chocolate**

**Chopped pistachios**

## MY METHOD

Combine flour, sugar, cocoa, cinnamon, and salt in the bowl of a stand mixer. Add wine or sherry and beat on low until dough just comes together. Use a rubber spatula to scrape down the sides.

Dump dough onto a lightly floured surface and knead until smooth and elastic, about 10 minutes. Cover with a clean dish towel and allow the dough to rest for 30 minutes.

Cut dough into 4 equal pieces using a sharp knife or bench scraper. Working with one piece at a time (keeping the other pieces covered loosely—flour them lightly and cover with a dish towel), begin passing the dough through the widest setting of a pasta machine and continue passing it through, narrowing the settings each time until it is as thin as you can get it. You can try your hand at using a rolling pin to achieve these results, but the pasta machine provides a more desired thinness.

Lay out the finished dough on a piece of parchment and cut first into squares about 4 × 4 inches. Then, cut each square diagonally into 2 even triangles.

Heat oil for frying to 365°F in a large, heavy-bottomed pot. Carefully fry the triangles in the oil for about 30 seconds or until they float to the top—you may need to encourage them with a gentle prod with some metal tongs or slotted-metal spoon. Flip it over and cook for another 15 seconds. Remove to a rack to cool. These can be made a day ahead, but are always best made fresh on the day you are going to serve them.

For serving, plate your triangles and dollop a generous spoonful of vanilla ricotta on top. Sprinkle with chocolate and pistachios. *Buon appetito*!

Special equipment: rolling pin or pasta machine

# THE GODFATHER

*Makes one cocktail*

I wanted to highlight Italy and how they have brought so much in the way of art, food, and familia to our country, and I am grateful for the delicious ways I can bring that culture into my home. Emma (my daughter) went to Rome this year and ate and drank her way through—bringing me back countless things she wanted me to prepare for her when she got home. I am all about creating a theme—it always makes things more memorable. This drink can be the beginning or the finish to such a theme—be it a *Soprano* themed birthday party, a *Godfather* movie binge, or just a way to gather la familia around the table for some time together.

Amaretto is a distinctly Italian liquor and thought to be a favorite of Marlon Brando, who played the title role of *The Godfather*. Serve this with the cannolis for a perfect after-dinner pair.

## INGREDIENTS

$1^{1}/16$ oz. Scotch whiskey
$1^{1}/16$ oz. Amaretto

## MY METHOD

Fill an old-fashioned glass with large ice cubes. Pour Scotch and Amaretto over ice. Gently swirl and serve.

# NORTH ATLANTIC ISLANDS

*Question 72: What non-volcanic islets, only about 80 feet above sea level, are found in the mid-Atlantic?*

*Question 73: What islands were used to determine the boundary line between Spanish and Portuguese colonization?*

*Question 74: What island has the world's oldest parliament?*

*Question 75: Spain and Portugal share the unusual situation of having their highest points offshore. In what island groups are the highest mountains in Spain and Portugal found?*

*Question 76: Where did the Bermuda onion originate?*

*Question 77: How do you make Beer-Battered Onion Rings?*

The earliest exploration of the world by Europeans began with the Atlantic Ocean. Probably this would have occurred in any case, but the existence of islands in the Atlantic made the process a whole lot easier. The Viking exploration of North America (for which they never got the press they deserved at the time—where were public relations firms when we really needed them?) used Iceland and Greenland as stepping stones. Columbus visited the Azores before he began. Vasco da Gama used both the Canary and the Cape Verde Islands en route to India.

Not all the Atlantic islands were stepping stones. Indeed, the ones I would most like to see are scarcely a dot in the ocean with no fresh water, nor even any vegetation. *The St. Peter and Paul Rocks in the mid-*

*Atlantic, roughly halfway between Brazil and Africa, are scarcely 80 feet above sea level at their highest point and are white, covered with guano.* Many a lookout in the days of sailing ships must have cried out "sail ho" since the Rocks resemble the white sails of a ship. I suppose one could consider them a true hazard to navigation in the early days of exploration, but they are located almost at the equator, where ships were often becalmed, or at least not going very fast. Moreover, their total land area is not much bigger than the surface of an aircraft carrier, so the odds of hitting them are small.

The St. Peter and Paul Rocks border on the miraculous. Almost all oceanic islands are volcanic. These rocks are not. Instead, they are the very tops of the mostly subterranean Atlantic oceanic ridge, the very long mountain range in the middle of the Atlantic. They are an oasis in the middle of nowhere, providing light for aquatic plants, which provide food for fish, which in turn attract sea birds. This tiny land area teems with life. The Rocks are owned by Brazil (I doubt there was much competition for sovereignty over them), which has built a small research station and lighthouse.

\* \* \*

The Cape Verde Islands, only 350 miles from the west African coast, provided the kind of stepping stones to exploration that we expect from Atlantic islands. They were claimed by early Portuguese explorers in the fifteenth century and became the very first tropical possession of a European nation. While the islands flourished in the days of the slave trade, economically they withered subsequently.

> Dr. G. says: A league is said to be three miles, but the measurement of land east and west (longitude) was so imprecise from shipboard that the actual location of the dividing line was mostly guesswork.

Long before the slave trade developed, however, *the Cape Verde Islands became famous as a point from which world dominion was to be shared between Spain and Portugal.* In 1493, a Spanish pope, Alexander VI, issued an edict that granted Spain all land west of a line running from pole to pole 100 leagues west of the Cape Verde Islands. Portugal was not mentioned in this edict, but Spain was given India in addition to the land west of the line.

Portugal was not satisfied with the division of the world by the pope. Their military power was sufficient to force reconsideration and the Treaty of Tordesillas, dividing the world between Spain and Portugal, was signed in 1494. The treaty set the dividing line between the colonial empires at 370 leagues west of the Cape Verde Islands. In effect, Portugal got all its holdings in Africa and Asia (including the pepper trade on the Malabar Coast of India) and Spain got the New World except for Brazil. The real prize was the Spice Islands (in modern Indonesia), which Portugal gained under the treaty but which Spain thought it had as a result of Columbus's voyages.

> Dr. G. says: Columbus kept insisting that he was just about to find the Spice Islands. In fact, he told his bosses, the dual monarchy of Spain, that he had seen the spice trees, but they weren't ripe at the time he was there.

\* \* \*

One of the largest Atlantic stepping stones was known simply as "The Island," but for some reason we have turned that name into "Iceland" in English. The first people there were probably Irish monks, but the first permanent settlement occurred in the ninth century by Vikings. Although Iceland is just south of the Arctic Circle, it is warmed by the Gulf Stream—early settlers depended on agriculture for their survival.

Iceland is an incredible place for many reasons (and a must for fledgling geographers to visit and study). Physically, it is at a conjunction of tectonic plates and produces both the explosive volcanoes characteristic of the Pacific Rim and the Mediterranean AND the basaltic volcanoes found in Hawaii. In fact, the north coast of Iceland looks remarkably like parts of the island of Hawaii—except for glaciers on the mountains. Historically, *Iceland was the origin of Viking exploration of Greenland and North America and the site of the world's oldest parliament, the Althing, established in 930 AD.*

*       *       *

One of my favorite geographic trivia question concerns the creature for which the Canary Islands was named. "Dog" is the correct answer, from the Latin word *"canus."* Since this now seems so widely known, perhaps a better question is: where do canaries come from? Actually, they do come from the Canary Islands, and are native also to Madeira and the Azores. So this little songbird is really named for a dog!

The native lands of the canary are the classic Atlantic stepping-stones: Madeira and the Canaries to the west coast of Africa, then on to India and Asia; the Azores to the Americas. Not surprisingly, these islands were contested by the first two exploring nations, Spain and Portugal. Columbus, who tried to get support for his voyages from both countries, married a woman from Madeira and visited the Azores before he began his series of exploring voyages. Eventually, Spain gained the Canaries and Portugal got the Azores (and Madeira).

*The Canary Islands are now part of Spain and, while a long way from the Iberian Peninsula, actually contain Spain's highest mountain, El Teide, on the island of Tenerife. Just as strange—and even further from Iberia—Portugal's highest mountain is in the Azores, Mount Pico on Pico Island.* The situation is somewhat familiar to Americans since their highest mountain is in Alaska!

\*  \*  \*

Bermuda is a mis-stepping-stone across the Atlantic. Some six hundred miles east of North Carolina, it would seem to be an ideal place for an exploring ship to stop and renew her water supply. Unfortunately, Bermuda is surrounded by reefs that prevent easy access; moreover, water is hard to come by. Even today, modern houses are built over cisterns and their roofs designed to catch rainfall. The Spanish came first to Bermuda, put a few pigs ashore, and never came back to settle or enforce their claim.

Bermuda became famous for the Bermuda onion, the first sweet onion to enter the American market. Bermuda has so little arable land that it seems impossible that it could become famous for any crop. Indeed, the Bermuda onion was eventually supplanted by other sweet onions grown in North America (such as Georgia's Vidalia onion). In any case, *the Bermuda onion is not native to Bermuda, but apparently to the Canary Islands.* "Bermuda onion" sounds much more attractive than "Canary onion"—truly a name for the birds.

*Bermuda (photo by bbf)*

# From Geography . . .

# . . . to Gastronomy

~

### Food for Thought
*"Onion rings in the car cushions do not improve with time."*
—Erma Bombeck

~

*Recipe for:*

Beer-Battered Onion Rings

# BEER-BATTERED ONION RINGS

*Makes 6–8 appetizer servings*

The first recipe for a battered onion ring first appeared in the *New York Times* in 1933. The obvious addition of a beer added to the batter was bound to follow—how can you not pair fried food with a rich, yeasty, dark brew? These are a bit labor intensive, but worth every step. Make sure to buy a few extra bottles of a nice dark porter to serve with these onion rings.

## INGREDIENTS

4 cups EVOO (or peanut or canola oil)

2 large Bermuda, Vidalia, Maui, or other sweet onions, cut into ½ inch slices

1 cup buttermilk or sour milk

1 egg

1¼ cups flour

1 teaspoon salt

1 teaspoon baking powder

2 teaspoons garlic powder

2 teaspoons paprika

1 cup panko

12 oz. beer (I use a porter)

## MY METHOD

Heat the oil in a Dutch oven to 365°F.

In a medium bowl, stir together the flour, salt, baking powder, garlic powder, and paprika.

Toss the onion slices in the flour mixture until they are coated, shaking them off gently, and setting aside on a baking sheet.

Make a well in the flour mixture and add in the beer, buttermilk, and egg. Gently whisk together using a fork. Allow to sit for 10 minutes.

Line a baking sheet with parchment and place a rack on the top.

Dip each flour-coated slice into the batter and place on the rack. The slices can overlap as you complete each one.

Spread the panko onto a shallow dish and coat each slice, scooping and pressing to get the panko to cling.

Deep fry a few at a time for 2–3 minutes or until golden brown. Remove with a slotted metal spoon and place on a rack on a baking sheet lined with paper towels to drain. Enjoy plain, with your favorite dipping sauce or with the **Cilantro-Lime Dipping Sauce** from chapter 14 or the **Garlic and Vanilla Aioli** from chapter 3.

# SOUTH ATLANTIC ISLANDS

*Question 78: What island group is called "Malvinas" by Argentina?*

*Question 79: On what island did Napoleon Bonaparte die?*

*Question 80: South Georgia and the South Sandwich Islands are a British territory; where are the Sandwich Islands?*

*Question 81: On what island group was the HMS* Rattlesnake *wrecked on October 21, 1781?*

*Question 82: What is the southernmost country in the world?*

*Question 83: What is the better-known name for the "Cape of Ovens"?*

*Question 84: How do you make Very English Tea Sandwiches?*

*The Falkland Islands were obscure to most of the world until the 1980s. At that time, the UK was negotiating with Argentina over the issue of the Falklands; Britain had claimed it as a colony, while Argentina considered it part of their sovereign territory. The Argentines called the islands the Malvinas.* The discovery and claims to the island group are muddled in the mists of history, but the bottom line was that the UK was spending a lot of money on the Falklands and seemed quite happy with the thought of dumping them on Argentina. Aside from some shipping facilities and herds of sheep, there was little of economic value there. There were, moreover, fewer than 3,000 inhabitants.

In April 1982, Argentina sent military forces to occupy the Falklands; Britain had no significant naval or military presence, so there was only slight resistance. The islands were sufficiently remote that the first confirmation of occupation by Argentina came from a ham radio operator in the Falklands. Notice that this occurred in fall in the Southern Hemisphere. The Argentines knew well that the generally bad weather that prevailed around the islands in the winter would deter counterattack by the British. Retaking the Falklands from Argentina was a very difficult military operation and things did not go smoothly for British forces, but they did succeed. Politically, this effectively destroyed the succession of military juntas that had ruled Argentina and ensured the reelection of the British Conservatives led by Margaret Thatcher.

One of the least known things about the war in the Falkland Islands was that it also restored British rule to South Georgia and the South Sandwich Islands. Also, a plebiscite was held in the Falklands in which 99.8 percent of the population opted for continued British rule.

Dr. G. says: South Georgia was retaken by British military operations, but Argentina had maintained control over the South Sandwich Islands for years while Britain attempted to regain them by diplomacy—the war resulted in the removal of all Argentine personnel from the South Sandwich Islands.

\*   \*   \*

Napoleon Bonaparte was really one of the strangest rulers in history. In the first place, he was a military leader who led the French to victory after victory (strange indeed). He also seems to have been perceived by the French as a savior of the values won in the French Revolution while at the same time exercising a tyranny that would have shamed the earlier Bourbon dynasty. He conquered or controlled virtually every major city in Europe (including Moscow, if briefly) except London, and only the Royal Navy (the same folks who

*St. Helena Island*

took back the Falkland Islands 170 years later) kept him from there. When *Napoleon was captured (twice) he was exiled, first on Elba (which didn't work out), then on St. Helena in the South Atlantic.*

Dr. G. says: A bonus trivia answer: St. Helena is the second oldest remaining British colony, after Bermuda.

St. Helena became an important British possession because of Britain's trade both with India and Australia. By the nineteenth century, sailing ships had discovered that going around either Cape Horn or the Cape of Good Hope was generally easier from the west (since the westerlies were the prevailing winds in those southern latitudes). No matter which route, however, St. Helena was ideally placed for ships returning to Britain from either Australia or India—and it was out of the way enough so that Napoleon was, well, out of the way. He died there on the fifth of May 1821.

South Georgia and the South Sandwich Islands would almost certainly be in Argentina's hands today had not their generals misjudged British resolve (and pride). In the early twentieth century, South Georgia's whaling port had been both the starting point and a salvation port for Ernest Shackleton's voyage in the *Endurance*. James Cook discovered and claimed the South Sandwich Islands in 1773, naming them "Sandwich Land" after the Earl of Sandwich, who was First Lord of the British Admiralty. Cook went on, however, to find another group of islands, this time in the mid-Pacific, which he called the "Sandwich Islands." To avoid confusion, the word "South" was added to the islands in the south Atlantic. *The Sandwich Islands in the Pacific were renamed the Hawaiian Islands.*

*      *      *

*Trindade and Martim Vaz Islands are an island group now part of Brazil. They occupy only about 4 square miles and currently have a population of thirty-two. They have, however, an interesting history. They were discovered by Edmond Halley, whose name comes up every seventy-six years or so. A British man of war, the HMS* Rattlesnake, *was wrecked on the shoals of these islands on October 21, 1781. The* Rattlesnake *was* there to survey the islands to see if a British base was feasible. The sloop-rigged cutter dragged anchor and nearly went aground. It escaped with remarkable seamanship but then hit a submerged rock off-shore and was beached to save its crew.

Trindade and Martim Vaz, however, became famous in the United States when an American claimed them and declared himself James I, military dictator of the islands. James Hardon-Hickey didn't stop at that, however. He had a flag made, along with a coat of arms, had stamps issued, and opened a consulate on W. 37th Street in New York. He dropped the *e* in Trindade but the scheme just didn't work out. Hardon-Hickey and his dictatorship faded away.

Dr. G. says: Pretentious trivia players and game-show hosts notwithstanding, no one is sure how the comet-discoverer's name was spelled, much less pronounced.

\* \* \*

Asking about the southernmost country in the world requires some rules (no Antarctic territory, for example) and elicits three answers: New Zealand, Chile, and Argentina. New Zealand is reasonable, but wrong, and Argentina (because the southernmost city in the world, Ushuaia, is in Argentina and has received a lot of publicity from cruise lines) is also wrong. *Chile is correct, and usually Cape Horn is cited as the southernmost point.*

Cape Horn was named by the Dutch after the city of Hoorn. It was easy to change "Hoorn" to "Horn," so many imagine that somehow either the island or its headland is horn-shaped. Neither are. *The final irony of the name is that the Chileans transposed "horn" to the Spanish word "hornos," which means "ovens." So, when you see Cabo de Hornos on a Spanish-language map, it means "cape of ovens."* Actually, there are some small islands southwest of Cape Horn in which pirates liked to lurk, hoping to intercept a valuable cargo, but the high seas, winds, and occasional ice flows meant this was not a good place for lurking. Whether the Diego Ramirez Islands should really be considered incidentally offshore, and hence a part of South America, or whether they are oceanic islands, is debatable (at least to me), but they are Chilean territory in any case.

# *From Geography . . .*

# *. . . to Gastronomy*

~

Food for Thought:

*"There are few hours in life more agreeable than the hour dedicated to the ceremony known as afternoon tea."*

—Henry James

~

*Recipe for:*

~~Very English Tea Sandwiches~~ **Rogue Pirate Picnic Sandwich**

# *Very English Tea Sandwiches*
# Rogue Pirate Picnic Sandwich

This one was one of those chapters where I looked at my dad and asked, "Really? I mean really?" With not a morsel mentioned, I have had to come up with a creative idea. So—here goes!

The Sandwich Islands are British, so I decided to write a recipe for the *very* British traditional tea sandwich, revered throughout the land for the afternoon ritual of slowing down after a hard day's work. Farmers would come in from the fields during the long summer hours to share a meal with their families and then head back out until the sun faded in the sky.

I then realized that I could never do justice to their sandwich because I always go rogue and don't adhere to the traditional "tea sandwich." I don't cut off the crusts or stick to one flavor, or for that matter use plain white bread at all (ever), in fact this is not a recipe for "sandwiches"—it is for one giant-sized sandwich.

So being rogue in a British protected area would be like a pirate, right? And pirates aren't civilized enough to have a tea party, but maybe they could have a picnic—because these sandwiches are big, chewy, on sourdough, bursting with lots of different flavors, and then pressed with a brick—sounds like a pirate picnic to me (or just a picnic with a lot of boys who don't have proper tea manners yet—which I swear I know nothing about!).

You can make this sandwich a day ahead—just don't add the feta spread until an hour before you serve it—you don't want it to get soggy, but you want time for the flavors to connect and the bread to get some of the flavors absorbed. For the bread, you want something that will have a bubbly, open crumb when you cut into it, but with a nice firm crust. You can use any shape or size loaf you want.

## INGREDIENTS

A large loaf of good, crusty bread

1 tablespoon Dijon mustard

3 tablespoons balsamic vinegar

½ cup EVOO

Salt and pepper to taste

½ cup olive paste, you may buy this prepared or you can make
  the recipe that follows

Eggplant sliced in ¼-inch-thick rounds, brushed with
  oil and baked at 350°F until browned and soft but not
  shriveling up, about 12–15 minutes

Marinated artichoke hearts, drained and rough chopped

Fresh spinach leaves, one bunch (about 2 cups)

Fresh basil, one bunch, sliced in chiffonade (about 1 cup)

Roasted bell peppers, 3 (recipe in chapter 14, page 141)

Feta cheese spread (recipe follows)

½ lb. prosciutto, thinly sliced

¼ lb. salami, thinly sliced

# OLIVE PASTE

## INGREDIENTS

½ cup black olives

½ cup green olives

½ cup Kalamata olives

1 tablespoon EVOO

2 teaspoons capers (rinsed if you find them too briny)

## MY METHOD

In a food processor with the blade, buzz together all of the olives with the EVOO. Stop machine and stir in 2 teaspoons capers. This is now ready for the sandwich. Reserve the remaining amount to go with crackers and cheese later. Or just bring them along for the picnic.

# FETA SPREAD

## INGREDIENTS

1 cup crumbled feta cheese
½ cup mayonnaise
1 teaspoon garlic powder
2 tablespoons apple cider vinegar

## MY METHOD

Combine all ingredients in a small bowl and set aside for at least one hour and up to 3 days in advance.

# ASSEMBLING THE SANDWICH

Slice open the loaf of bread lengthwise so that there is one big top piece and one big bottom piece. Cut or pull out the center parts of the loaf (perfect to use with the remaining olive paste).

You can layer it anyway you want, but here's how I do it, bottom first:

Olive paste
Half of the spinach
Eggplant
Bell peppers
Artichokes
Half of the basil
Half of the feta spread
Salami
Prosciutto
Remaining feta spread
Remaining spinach
Remaining basil

Spread a layer of olive paste over the bottom piece. Add half of the spinach, then the eggplant, then bell peppers, then artichokes, then half of the basil, then half of the feta spread. Add in layers of the salami and prosciutto. Spread the remaining feta spread on the meat and layer the remaining spinach and basil. Place the top of the bread on sandwich.

Wrap tightly in parchment paper or aluminum foil (you may want to double wrap it). If you are using parchment, seal it with masking tape. Place the sandwich on a baking sheet and set a large cast-iron skillet on top. Sometimes I will add extra weight (like a couple of big cans of tomatoes) and set it in the skillet to assist in pressing the sandwich. Allow it to sit for at least an hour, and no more than two.

Unwrap, slice, and enjoy! Or argh matey!

# WORLD HOT SPOTS

*Question 85: What is the oldest language in Europe and where is it spoken?*

*Question 86: During the Korean War (or Conflict), where did US troops make a seaborne landing that outflanked North Korean forces?*

*Question 87: What was the name given to the area colonized by France and from which the countries of Vietnam, Cambodia, and Laos were created?*

*Question 88: What country borders Mexico on the south?*

*Question 89: What Central American country was considered as an alternative to Panama for a canal to connect the Atlantic and Pacific?*

*Question 90: What river separates Buda from Pest, the two parts of Hungary's capital?*

*Question 91: How do you make Sweet Pepper and Onion Jam and Christmas Eve Wings with Cilantro-Lime Dipping Sauce?*

Some places are hardly ever in the news, while others—so-called "hot spots"—seem to be in the headlines frequently. Terrorism, revolution, or even outright war characterizes these prominent places. Ideally, there would be a required geography course in high school that dealt with such areas so that Americans could be better informed about the foundations (or lack thereof) of US foreign policy regarding chronic trouble spots.

Some hot spots have been around for hundreds of years with only brief interruptions of violence and political instability, while others turn "hot" only intermittently. One perennial hot spot is the region between France and Spain, called the "Basque Country." The larger and more prosperous portion of the Basque Country is in Spain, while the French side appears to be growing ever more prosperous by the immigration of successful Basque people from all over the world who have returned to their homeland, often for retirement. The French side is, in my opinion, one of the most beautiful places in the world. The Basque people have been seeking recognition as a separate nation for a long, long time. This had led to severe violence, most of it in Spain. While currently the situation has cooled, the rising nationalism that has been witnessed in Scotland and in another part of Spain, Catalonia, makes it more likely that Basque separatism will again make headlines in the future.

ETA is the militant arm of Basque separatists. Since its foundation in the 1950s, ETA has morphed into new organizations and objectives. In 2011, ETA declared a "ceasefire"; prior to that time, however, it killed over 800 people in terrorist attacks. Current public opinion polls show minimal support for ETA among the Basque people.

*Basque is almost certainly the oldest language in Europe* and is unrelated to any other European language. Several symbols and landmarks are characteristic of the Basque Country, but probably none is more common and familiar than the red pepper—called "pimiento" in the region. Clusters of peppers hang from Basque homes and businesses. The irony of this is that the peppers are not native to the Basque Country but originated in the New World.

Columbus brought back the chili pepper, or pimiento, with him from the New World, along with other flora (such as corn, potato, chocolate, and vanilla), but it was centuries before they became important products in Europe.

\*    \*    \*

Korea was once referred to as the "hermit kingdom." The Korean Peninsula is between two perennial East Asian military powers: Japan and China. To preserve its way of life, Korean society embraced isolation and stressed cultural and racial purity. Korea's mountainous terrain also discouraged military invasion. In 1910, however, Japan annexed Korea and retained possession until the end of World War II.

During World War II, the Japanese sent 400,000 Koreans to work in Japan as part of the war effort; many of them became coal miners. Eventually, the Koreans took Japanese names and, to some extent, assimilated into Japanese society. Korean businesses in Japan, however, commonly identify themselves to other Koreans by a display of stylized red peppers on their signs and doors. Red chilies and chili paste are traditional ingredients in Korean cuisine.

Korea was divided into North and South Korea after the defeat of Japan in 1945. The invasion of South Korea by North Korean forces in 1950 pushed South Korean and US forces almost to the end of the Korean Peninsula. *General MacArthur, however, ordered a seaborne landing on Korea's west coast at Inchon, a move that essentially outflanked the North Korean invaders* and turned the tide of the war. Despite an armistice agreement in 1953, North Korea insists that it is still at war. The border between the two countries thus remains one of the world's hottest spots.

*       *       *

*Indochina was the name given to the French colonial area of Southeast Asia*, and it is an appropriate name in the sense that the region has been heavily influenced by both China and India. The area remains unstable today, with real or potential conflict between and among national groups (particularly along border regions), tribal groups, and religious groups. Islam, Buddhism, and some Hinduism are found in the region, and a veneer of Christianity also exists in several places.

Some political observers believe that several "flash points" exist in Southeast Asia that could turn into major conflicts at any time. East Timor, once a colony of Portugal, has become essentially a Christian enclave in a Muslim country (Indonesia). East Timor

has gone through periods of proclaimed independence, occupation by Indonesian troops, and independence again, by plebiscite.
Some estimates indicate as many as 200,000 people died in the
violence during Indonesian occupation—this out a population of
about 800,000. Indonesia also contends with a violent independence movement in the mineral-rich area of western New Guinea.
Vietnam, Laos, and Cambodia have all experienced brutal civil wars.
Perhaps the most volatile current flash point is in southern Thailand
where Islamic separatists battle the Thai military.

Southeast Asia was colonized by three European powers: the
Dutch (the East Indies, now Indonesia, excluding parts of Borneo),
the English (Burma, now called Myanmar by some, Malaya, now
Malaysia and Singapore), and the French (Indochina). Within the
region, only Siam (now Thailand) was never colonized. As is the case
with sub-Saharan Africa, the colonizers drew boundaries for their
own convenience with little regard for the reality of the homelands
of many different groups. With independence, the newly emerged
states were a jumble of different languages, religions, and tribal
groups. We can expect political instability in the region into the
indefinite future.

The chili pepper is, strangely, one of the things that unifies the
cuisine, and hence the culture, of Southeast Asia. Although it has
not become a cultural icon (as in Korea and the Basque Country), it
is nevertheless commonly used. Thai restaurants, which have become
common in North America and Europe, often feature menus with
"hot, medium, or mild" variations in individual dishes, depending
on the amount of chilies used. My personal (albeit limited) experience has been that Burmese cooking uses peppers even more extensively than does Thai cooking.

\* \* \*

*Mexico's neighbor to the south is Guatemala.* It became one of the CIA's first
Latin American targets when, during the Eisenhower administra-

tion, a decision was made to overthrow the government of President
Jacobo Arbenz. In 1944, a popular uprising had overthrown one of
the most oppressive dictatorships in Latin America and instituted
democratic reforms, including land reform. Arbenz was elected
president in 1950 and continued the reforms. The CIA, led by Allen
Dulles, determined that Guatemala was a Soviet puppet state.

The coup staged by the Eisenhower administration through the
CIA plunged Guatemala into a civil war that lasted nearly half a
century. The ever-changing conflict involved a rural, Indian (many
Mayans) peasantry against the military, supported and trained by the
United States. While things have stabilized since 1996, Guatemala
remains one of the world's potential hot spots—as well as an area
where chili peppers have been cultivated for 5,000 years or longer.

*   *   *

When the Americans decided to finish the work that the French
had begun on the Panama Canal, *they gave serious consideration to building
an Atlantic-Pacific connection through Nicaragua.* Because Nicaragua had two
large freshwater lakes that could be used as part of a canal system, it
would be cheaper and easier to build there. Nicaragua, however, had
several active volcanoes that the US government felt could destroy a
canal. Ironically, the eventual plans for a canal in Panama called for
changing the topography of Panama to resemble Nicaragua's—but
without the volcanoes!

The Panama Canal was very difficult to build. In part, the design of the canal was a major issue. There was a continual argument
among design engineers about whether the canal should be sea level
(as was the Suez Canal) or whether locks should be built. The French
were committed to a sea-level canal, as were the Americans when they
first took on the project. There seems to be a consensus today among
contemporary engineers that a sea-level canal (lockless) would have
been impossible.

*Panama Canal (photo by bbf)*

New canal locks are being constructed and are expected to be open for operation by 2016. Meanwhile, a Chinese company has contracted with the Nicaraguan government to build a canal through that country that will compete with the Panama Canal. The company began construction at the end of 2014 and plans to complete the project in five years.

Both Panama and Nicaragua are global political "hot spots" where the United States has repeatedly intervened. They are also countries where the chili pepper is a culinary mainstay.

*       *       *

Hungary became a modern "hot spot" in 1956 when its uprising against Soviet domination attracted worldwide attention. While the revolt was put down by a massive Soviet force, it eventually led to

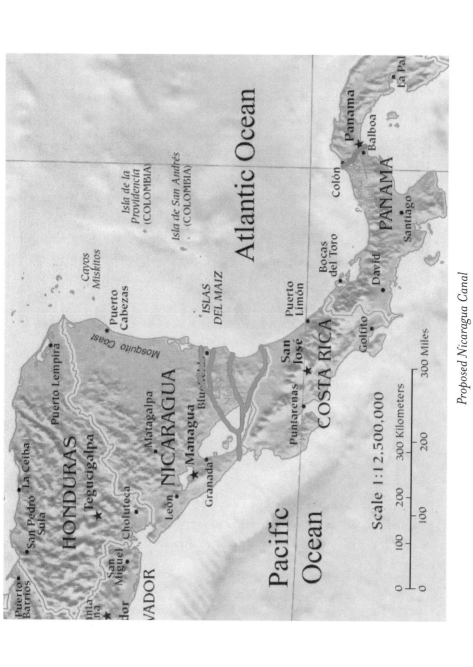

*Proposed Nicaragua Canal*

some reform of the Communist regime that had been in place since the end of WWII. The uprising is cited as one of the earliest "cracks" in the Iron Curtain and a forerunner of the eventual collapse of Soviet domination of Eastern Europe.

Hungary is an anomaly in Europe because its language is not European, but rather Uralic. The Hungarians, who use the word "Magyar" to refer to themselves, originated east of the Ural Mountains and moved westward into Europe and were well established there by 900 CE. They are the largest group in Europe to speak a non-Indo-European language.

*The capital of Hungary, Budapest, consists of two separate cities, Buda and Pest, which are divided by the Danube River.* If the city is divided, the cuisine is unified by the use of several different varieties of paprika. Paprika is essentially dried and ground chili peppers.

\*   \*   \*

Why is the chili pepper widely used and even emblematic in areas as diverse as Korea, Hungary, the Basque region, Central America, and Southeast Asia? Or, put another way, why did the chili pepper not make such a major impact on the cuisines of France, Italy, and Greece? Why not England? ("English cuisine" is an oxymoron, which is why I don't use the term here.) I have no answer, but simply the observation that hot pepper sauces are now so commonly used in the United States that they have joined ketchup and mustard in the condiment array found on dining tables.

> Dr. G. says: A famous anthropologist has claimed that dairy products consumed in Northern Europe somehow blunted the taste of chilies and thus limited their use.

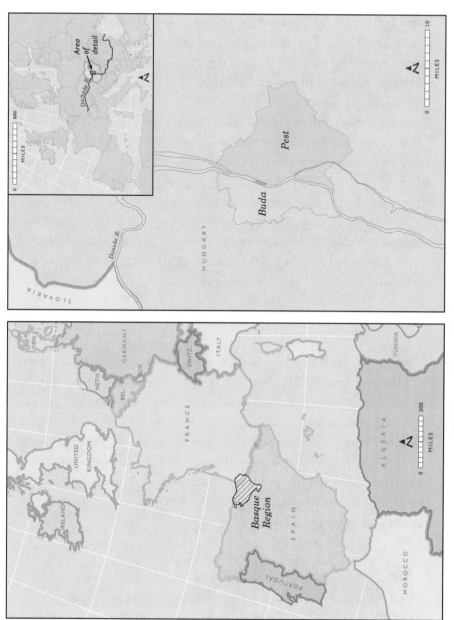

*The Basque Country/Budapest and the Danube*

# From Geography . . .

## . . . to Gastronomy

~

Food for Thought:

*"There is no love sincerer than the love of food."*

—George Bernard Shaw

~

## Recipes for:

Sweet Pepper and Onion Jam
Christmas Eve Wings with Cilantro-Lime Dipping Sauce

# SWEET PEPPER AND ONION JAM

*Makes about 2 cups*

This is one of my family's favorites. It can be eaten on crostini accompanied with a smear of garlicky aioli or creamy goat cheese, paired with grilled ribeye, roasted pork loin, or fish tacos, and also is superb in an omelet with Boursin cheese and chives. I never seem to make enough, so you might want to double the batch. You can make a relish by finely chopping your ingredients—and I have had this on a sweet roll with a polish sausage (which makes an incredible gourmet hot dog), but I like the bigger, chunkier bites, so I chop everything into medium-sized pieces. For those of you who would like to try your hand at roasting your own peppers, the recipe follows below.

## INGREDIENTS

3 tablespoons EVOO

2 large onions, medium chopped

4 sweet bell peppers (red, orange, or yellow), roasted and peeled, then chopped into medium pieces

4 cloves garlic, thinly sliced

3 tablespoons sherry vinegar

1 tablespoon vanilla extract

2 tablespoons pimenton (smoked paprika)

## MY METHOD

In a large, heavy-bottomed skillet, heat oil on medium-low heat. Add onions, cover and sweat them for 5–7 minutes until soft. Remove cover, raise heat to medium and continue cooking, stirring occasionally. When they begin to caramelize and turn golden brown, add garlic and stir for one minute. Then add in peppers. Cook for another 3 minutes, stirring. Create a well in the center of your pan by pushing the vegetables toward the sides. Pour your sherry vinegar and vanilla into the well. Add in pimenton and stir well, allowing all of the flavors to combine. Cook until most of the liquid is absorbed, 5–7 minutes. Enjoy warm, or refrigerate for up to one week.

# HOW TO ROAST A BELL PEPPER

Since you are using a lot of energy from your oven, why not make a big batch for other recipes? They freeze nicely and can be used for soups, omelets, sandwiches, and stir-frys.

Preheat oven to 450°F.

Slice bell peppers in half. Devein and remove seeds.

Place peppers skin side up on a parchment–lined baking sheet.

Bake for 20–25 minutes or until skin is charred and blackened. Remove from oven.

Using tongs, place charred peppers into a paper bag and roll the top of the bag to enclose the peppers inside to allow them to sweat.

Once they have cooled (about 10–15 minutes), tear open the bag and peel or rub off the skins.

# CHRISTMAS EVE WINGS WITH CILANTRO-LIME DIPPING SAUCE

Every Christmas Eve, our family has a traditional meal of these wings, paired with a garlicky Christmas Fettuccine and a Thai Caesar Salad. The flavor of these wings has a Cuban-Asian feel to them, blending the spicy sriracha with cumin and oregano (and of course, mellow vanilla to smooth them all out) paired with the cool cilantro lime to soothe your palate. Sriracha can be found in the Asian section of your grocery store. It is a spicy sauce from the coastal city of Si Racha in Chonburi province of east Thailand.

If you can, I recommend marinating them over night—it really does make a difference. The dipping sauce should also be made the day ahead to allow the flavors to combine. You can bake the wings if you like—just omit the frying portion of the recipe and skip to the baking part, adding 5–10 minutes onto the baking time. We always end up frying them though since we live by the mantra that "everything is better fried!"

## INGREDIENTS

10 lbs. chicken wings (whole wings with both joints, not the "party wings")

1 tablespoon ground cumin

1 teaspoon ground oregano

1 tablespoon vanilla extract

2 tablespoons kosher salt

⅓ cup EVOO

1–1½ cups tapioca flour (or cornstarch)

Oil for frying, I use EVOO, but peanut or vegetable is fine

16 tablespoons salted butter (Kerrygold is best)

1 cup sriracha sauce

2 tablespoons brown sugar

## MY METHOD

The night before (or at least 4 hours), marinate the chicken in cumin, oregano, vanilla, salt, and olive oil. Turn to coat evenly and refrigerate, turning them occasionally to marinate all sides of the chicken.

Remove from marinade and place on baking sheets lined with racks. Allow them to drip dry a bit.

Preheat oven to 425°F. In a large, heavy-bottomed skillet, heat oil to 360°F for olive oil, 375°F for peanut or vegetable.

In a brown paper bag, add ½ cup of tapioca or cornstarch. Add chicken in batches of 4–6 and shake them in the bag to coat with starch, adding more starch as needed.

Fry wings until golden brown, turning to fry evenly.

Remove and place on rack.

Once all wings are fried, place them in oven and cook for 10–15 minutes at 375°F until cooked through.

While the wings are baking, melt butter in a saucepan and add sriracha and brown sugar. Stir until sugar dissolves and keep warm.

When wings are fully cooked, dip each into the sriracha sauce and serve on a platter with cilantro-lime dipping sauce. I like to have a gravy boat of the sriracha sauce on the table for those of us who like a little more sauce.

# CILANTRO-LIME DIPPING SAUCE

## INGREDIENTS

1 bunch cilantro (about 1 cup), chopped

1 cup mayonnaise

½ cup sour cream

½ cup feta cheese, crumbled

2 limes, zested and juiced

½ teaspoon *patis* (fish sauce)

## MY METHOD

Stir together all ingredients in a small bowl. Cover and refrigerate for at least one hour or overnight.

*Christmas Eve wings (photo by bbf)*

# RELIGIOUS MOVEMENTS

*Question 92: What colony and later US state was founded by a member of the Religious Society of Friends?*

*Question 93: What three Anabaptist groups settled in large numbers in the United States and Canada?*

*Question 94: What religious group originated in England, settled first in Mt. Lebanon, New York, and demanded celibacy of its members?*

*Question 95: What US state, originally settled by a religious dissident, has the longest name?*

*Question 96: Which state, originally a haven for Roman Catholics fleeing from England, ended up denying Catholics the right to vote and restricting their immigration until 1820?*

*Question 97: How do you make Dad's Thanksgiving Stuffing and Amish Chicken?*

The earliest settlers in what is now the United States were English—no surprise, since we were English colonies! It is commonly believed that these earliest settlers came for religious freedom. While that is not always the case, it is a reasonable generalization. By 1620, when the Pilgrims settled at Plymouth, England had undergone more than a century of religious turmoil, featuring civil war, revolution, and regicide. A religious group favored and protected during one monarch's reign might be persecuted by the successor to the throne.

Dr. G. says: The Pilgrims were not seeking religious freedom; they had that in the Netherlands. Their migration can be called a commercial deal from which a profit was expected.

One religious group that came to America to avoid persecution was the Religious Society of Friends, commonly known as the Quakers. The Quakers are interesting for several reasons. Unlike other small groups from either England or Europe, the Quakers continued to exist and grow in their homeland after some of their members migrated to the New World; in fact, more than 1 percent of the population of England and Wales were Quakers in 1680, even as Quakers had begun to settle mainly in two American colonies: Rhode Island and Pennsylvania. *Pennsylvania was one of the largest land grants ever and was given to a Quaker, William Penn.*

By the early nineteenth century, Quakers declined in numbers, both in the United States and in Great Britain. Disputes and new theologies and practices splintered the group. The influence, both political and economic, that the Quakers had in colonial times evaporated. Ironically, however, the only US president who was a Quaker was elected in the twentieth century—Richard Nixon.

News programs and TV script writers often confuse Quakers with other religious groups that settled in Pennsylvania, particularly the Mennonites and Amish. The former were English; the latter two, generally German. The term "Pennsylvania Dutch" refers to German settlers, not the Quakers.

Dr. G. says: "Pennsylvania Dutch" comes from the German word for German: *deutsch*.

\* \* \*

*The Mennonites and Amish are derived* from Anabaptist groups that emerged during the Protestant Reformation in Germany, Switzerland, and the Netherlands. Both groups were named after their founders: Menno Simon and Jakob Ammann. The Amish, most famously residing in Lancaster County, Pennsylvania, have grown significantly in numbers and are now found in several areas of the United States. They no longer exist in their European homeland. *Another Anabaptist group, the Hutterites* (also named after their founder, Jakop Hutter) settled in the Dakotas and the Canadian Prairie Provinces. The Hutterites are often cited by population geographers and other demographic experts because their birthrate is probably the world's highest.

Dr. G. says: Anabaptist refers to the belief that, since early Christians were adults, infant baptism should not be practiced; it was viewed as a "forced conversion."

\* \* \*

Another small English religious group *the Shakers, first settled in Mt. Lebanon, New York,* and later established other settlements in New England. They were well-known for two things: 1) their inventions and handcrafted items, especially furniture; and 2) their vows of celibacy which went a long way to explaining why their population has declined. There is only one Shaker community left in the United States, and it has only three members.

\* \* \*

It is highly ironic that the colony, and later US state, with probably the greatest religious tolerance and the first to ban slavery was also the leading slave-trading colony. Roger Williams was a Cambridge-educated theologian who migrated to the Puritan colony at Boston, but came to distance himself entirely from the Church of England. As a Separatist, he found refuge initially among the Pilgrims at Plymouth, but later moved to an area on Narragansett Bay outside the boundaries of original colonial grants. His colony was called Providence Plantations and later joined with the neighboring colony of Rhode Island. The resulting state was named *Rhode Island and the Providence Plantations, which is the longest name of any state.* In 2012, voters were given the opportunity to change the state's name officially to the more familiar "Rhode Island"; they opted for the longer name.

\*　\*　\*

When we think about people migrating to the New World to find religious freedom, we tend to think about small religious communities like the Pilgrims, Quakers, and Amish. Roman Catholics, however, who had been THE Christian group in Europe prior to the Reformation, also suffered from severe persecution at various times in Britain and Europe. Maryland was created by a grant from Charles I to George Calvert, a Catholic who desired a place of refuge for English Catholics. Calvert also had profit in mind; his initial colonial venture in Newfoundland had failed, and he hoped to produce tobacco. Calvert died before the first settlers arrived, but his son, Cecil, continued the settlement plan. The first colonists arrived in 1633. With the passage of time, however, other religious groups moved to Maryland until Catholics became a small minority. While it's not easy to measure religious persecution on a scale, it is not unreasonable to claim that, by the late seventeenth century, persecution of Catholics was more severe in Maryland than in most colonies. Catholics were denied the right to vote, and Maryland passed laws restricting Catholic settlement that lasted until 1820.

Dr. G. says: While the Calvert family may not have realized their financial aspirations in early Maryland, things worked out well in the long run. Maryland is now the richest US state as measured by per capita income.

# From Geography . . .

*Amish buggy (photo by "Utente: TheCadExpert")*

## . . . to Gastronomy

~

Food for Thought:

*"Kissing wears out. Cooking don't."*

—Amish saying

~

**Recipes for:**

Dad's Thanksgiving Stuffing
Amish Chicken

# DAD'S THANKSGIVING STUFFING

Living in Hawaii gives us the privilege of combining the flavors of many different cultures that truly make this place a melting pot. Please enjoy this ono (delicious) stuffing that my family has enjoyed for generations. To learn about the Portuguese in Hawaii and about the pao doce, or sweet bread, they brought, visit the website of the Kona Historical Society. The **challah** from chapter 19 works nicely here as well.

Use with a 20 pound turkey.

## INGREDIENTS

2 lbs. Portuguese pao doce (sweet bread)

1½ lbs. Portuguese sausage, chopped

8 tablespoons butter

2 medium onions, diced

6 stalks celery, diced

I cup macadamia nuts, chopped and lightly toasted

2 tablespoons poultry seasoning

4–6 cups low-sodium chicken or vegetable broth

## GRANDMA'S METHOD

Break bread into bite-sized chunks and spread out on baking sheets. Place in oven overnight (no heat) to dry out a bit.

In a large stockpot over medium heat, cook sausage until the fat is rendered and sausage is nicely browned (we use Redondo's mild, although any Linguiça or chorizo would be good). With a slotted spoon, remove sausage and place onto a plate lined with paper towels. Press firmly with more paper towels to press out fat. Once it has cooled, carefully pour out the rendered fat from stockpot into a glass jar for disposal.

In the same stockpot, return heat to medium and add butter, onion, and celery. Cook, stirring often, 8–10 minutes, or until vegetables are softened and beginning to brown. Add poultry sea-soning and stir for another minute. Remove from heat.

Add to the pot half of the sweet bread and half of the sausage. Stirring to combine, moisten with some of the broth until the bread begins to hold together (too much will make it mushy!). Add the remaining bread and sausage. Moisten again with broth. Toss in macadamia nuts and stir to combine.

Preheat the oven to 350°F. Place the stuffing mixture in but-tered baking dishes and bake until heated through and brown on top, 30–45 minutes, or stuff into your turkey and bake according to directions.

*Amish chicken (photo by bbf)*

# AMISH CHICKEN

*Serves 8*

I first made this in high school—my dad found the recipe in the newspaper, and we cut it out and saved it. It was an instant family favorite. I don't know what we liked better—the crispy skin on the chicken or the garlicky morsels of delight. The tender garlic and cream makes the perfect gravy to go with mashed potatoes, egg noodles, or a fluffy rice pilaf. For a vegetable, green beans with browned butter and sliced almonds, or try the **Pea Salad** recipe in chapter 21.

## INGREDIENTS

8 chicken thighs

Garlic cloves, as many or as few as you like (I usually put 20–30), peeled

1 cup all-purpose flour

1 tablespoon paprika

1 tablespoon garlic powder

1 tablespoon salt

1 teaspoon white pepper

1 quart heavy cream

1 quart chicken stock

## MY METHOD

In a large bowl, combine flour, paprika, garlic powder, salt, and pepper. Dredge chicken and shake off excess. Place chicken in a large baking dish, skin side up. Pour in cream and stock. Distribute garlic around the chicken.

Bake at 350°F for 60 minutes or until the skin of the chicken is crispy and browned.

# SOUTH OF THE BORDER

Question 98: What is celebrated in Mexico on May 5th (Cinco de Mayo)?

Question 99: What is the only Central American country without a Caribbean (or Atlantic) coastline?*

Question 100: What US state capital is almost exactly due north of the Mexican resort, Cozumel?

Question 101: In what Central American country is English the official language?

Question 102: What national capital is closest to the US naval base at Guantanamo Bay?

Question 103: How do you make Crab Enchilada Bake with Red and White Sauces?

I never heard of most Mexican food until I was well into adulthood. Things like tacos, enchiladas, tortas, and burritos were completely unknown in my neck of the woods. A possible exception was chili con carne. I'm not sure if this is a Mexican dish or not. It certainly was a staple in Texas by the end of the nineteenth century and had spread to the Midwest United States by the early twentieth century. Outside Texas, Cincinnati was probably best known as a font of chili con carne, but St. Louis and Green Bay also have some claim. All chili recipes seem unique, and cooks are highly pretentious about their particular version. In the Midwest, it is common to serve chili over spaghetti, while in Hawaii it is poured over rice. Because of the variations in recipes, chili contests are often held.

> Dr. G. says: My mother and father ran a small Adirondack hotel in the late 1940s. One winter, my mother added chili to the menu at 25 cents a bowl. She never could make enough; it was sold out every day. There were seemingly dozens of suggestions about ingredients that would improve the dish, but the most common was Tabasco sauce. This was, at that time, a storied condiment, but unavailable from any suppliers or nearby groceries. Her recipe used ground bear meat and cloves. Whenever I eat chili, I miss the subtle flavor of cloves.

Since my youth, aspects of Mexican culture, especially its alleged cuisine, have spread to all parts of the United States. Along with food, Mexican beers and tequila have become very popular in the United States. A few Spanish words have also crept into the vocabulary of many Americans. Perhaps the most pervasive aspect of Mexican culture in the US is the celebration of Cinco de Mayo. The trouble is that Cinco de Mayo is not Mexican Independence Day as is commonly believed in the United States. Independence Day is a huge holiday in Mexico and is celebrated on September 16. On that day, in the small town of Dolores (near Guanajuato), Father Hidalgo issued an appeal for independence from Spain. This event, called the *Grito de Independencia* (or *Grito de Dolores*) is repeated every year by the president of Mexico.

The fifth of May is a Mexican holiday, not as important as Independence Day, but still significant. *It celebrates the Mexican victory at the Battle of Puebla* where a powerful French army of 6,000 was defeated by a Mexican army of half its size. As impressive as the victory was, it accomplished little. The French stayed on in Mexico and installed

Maximillian as emperor. It seems to me that the celebration of Cinco de Mayo is a much bigger event in the United States than it is in Mexico.

* * *

El Salvador is the smallest country in Central America, but with the highest population density. Like much of Central America, it is topped with volcanoes and has frequent earthquakes. Its soils and general growing conditions proved ideal for coffee production and, in the recent past, El Salvador's economy was almost entirely dependent on coffee. Like any one-crop economy, the country was greatly affected by world market fluctuations, so "boom to bust" characterized their situation. In colonial days, El Salvador also specialized in one crop: indigo. Partially because of dependence on one crop, El Salvador has a history of great economic and political instability, replete with civil wars, battles of the military versus the peasantry, and guerilla insurgencies. Politically, things have been relatively calm for the last two decades. Weather-wise, *El Salvador has experienced some heavy Pacific storms in recent years. It has no Caribbean coast—the only country in Central America to lack direct access to the Atlantic.* Generally, it is out of the belt of Caribbean hurricanes, but is quite vulnerable to hurricanes that develop in the eastern Pacific (and which usually don't make the national news in the United States).

A student of mine was planning on flying to Los Angeles, renting a car, and driving to an environmental conference in Cozumel, Mexico. I gently suggested that this was some drive, perhaps the better part of 2,000 miles (I didn't actually measure it). He got a certain look in his eye—the same look one gets after watching Fox News. That is, he was highly dubious. He explained that he'd been to Mexico, just south of San Diego, not much of a drive at all. I told him Cozumel was just about due south of a US state capital. To his credit, he suggested Sacramento and Phoenix—both of which are actually state capitals. In truth, *the correct answer is Montgomery, Alabama.*

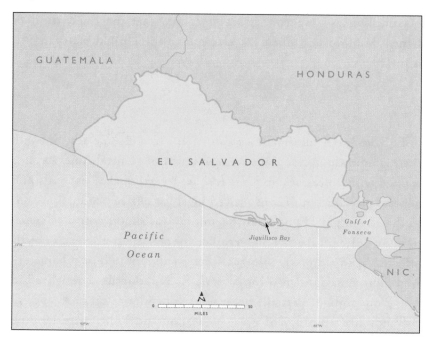

*El Salvador*

Americans in general have an image of Mexico that exaggerates its position to the west. Mexico's Yucatan Peninsula is geologically the same formation that has created Florida.

\*  \*  \*

Can a country actually be founded by pirates? In the case of Belize, that's pretty close to the truth. All of Central America was once part of that area known as New Spain. Nevertheless, Spain had little interest in the territory we now call Belize. It had no gold or silver, and it seemed unsuitable for most agriculture. It was indeed a backwater area, but ideal as a base for Caribbean pirates. Most of these pirates were originally from the British Isles; in fact, many learned their trade as part of the British Navy, but piracy paid better—at least until the British Navy decided to put pirates out of business in the Caribbean. Yet the beached pirates and their descendants could still furnish forest products to the British. *Although Belize's modern population is similar in many respects to other Central American countries, English remains the national language*—a feature that makes it attractive to American, Canadian, and British retirees.

*       *       *

"Gitmo," the Navy's nickname for its base at Guantanamo Bay, Cuba, has been in the news, off and on, for most of the Obama administration. The United States is faced with a dilemma: it has captured prisoners in a non-war from an enemy that doesn't exist, or better put, from an enemy that exists primarily in virtual space. There is no country to negotiate with, no country in real space with which to exchange prisoners. Were these non-prisoners of war taken to the United States, they presumably would come under US law, or at least under international law. By keeping them at Gitmo, the US is storing them (almost) in the "cloud."

The United States acquired Guantanamo Bay initially with its victory in the Spanish-American War, then by treaty when Cuba gained its (nominal) independence in 1902. Cuba's informal national anthem is taken from a poem by Cuban hero Jose Marti, *"Guantanamera,"* which refers to a woman from Guantanamo Bay. *"Gitmo" is closer to Kingston, Jamaica, than it is to Havana—and closer also to Port-au-Prince, Haiti.*

Dr. G. says: Under the treaty, the United States was allowed to intervene in Cuba whenever US officials thought it necessary.

# *From Geography . . .*

## *. . . to Gastronomy*

~

### Food for Thought:

*"If you really want to make a friend, go to someone's house and eat with him . . . the people who give you their food, give you their heart."*

—Cesar Chavez

~

### *Recipe for:*

Crab Enchilada Bake with Red and White Sauces

# CRAB ENCHILADA BAKE WITH RED AND WHITE SAUCES

*Serves 6*

## ENCHILADA INGREDIENTS

I lb. crab meat, picked through, removing cartilage, and
blotted dry with paper towels

I lb. cheddar/jack cheese blend, shredded, reserving ½ cup
for sprinkling over the top

I bunch (about 6–8 individual) green onions, both green and
white parts, sliced

12 small corn tortillas (white or yellow)

2 tablespoons unsalted butter, melted

Red sauce (see recipe below)

White sauce (see recipe below)

One bunch fresh cilantro, chopped

## MY METHOD

Assembling the enchilada bake:

In a large bowl, combine the crab meat, shredded cheese, and
green onions. Mix well.

Arrange 6 of the corn tortillas (cutting them if needed) to line the
bottom of a 9 X 12 baking dish. Brush with butter.

Spoon the white sauce over the tortillas.

Layer the crab mixture on top of the white sauce and cover with
the remaining tortillas.

Pour the red sauce over the top of the tortillas and sprinkle reserved cheese.

Bake at 375° F for 30 minutes until cooked through and bubbly.
The edges of the tortillas should be slightly crisped.

Allow to cool for at least 15 minutes. Cut into squares and remove
with a square spatula. Top with fresh cilantro.

Serve with refried beans, Spanish rice, and crisp green salad
drizzled with a red wine vinaigrette.

## RED SAUCE INGREDIENTS

3 tablespoons EVOO
1 tablespoon flour
¼ cup chili powder
1 teaspoon ground oregano
1 tablespoon ground cumin
¼ teaspoon cayenne pepper or a few dashes of your favorite
   hot sauce (optional)
2 cups chicken or vegetable stock
10 oz. tomato paste
Salt and pepper to taste

## MY METHOD

To make red sauce, add oil in a medium saucepan over medium heat. Sprinkle in flour and stir, cooking until it turns slightly golden.

Add in spices and continue cooking, stirring for another minute.

Pour in stock and tomato paste and cook for 12–15 minutes to thicken. Add salt and pepper to taste.

## WHITE SAUCE INGREDIENTS

1 cup half and half
½ cup sour cream
¼ cup unsalted butter

## MY METHOD:

Add all ingredients in small saucepan and heat over low until butter is melted, stirring to blend.

# THE LAND DOWN UNDER US

*Question 104: What name did Columbus give to Cuba?*

*Question 105: What territory did Britain trade for Cuba?*

*Question 106: What US battleship blew up in Havana Bay?*

*Question 107: Who was overthrown when Fidel Castro came to power?*

*Question 108: Where was the unsuccessful invasion that attempted to overthrow Castro?*

*Question 109: What do Che Guevara, Butch Cassidy, and the Sundance Kid have in common?*

*Question 110: How do you make Arroz con Pollo?*

Cuba has been much in the news since the Obama administration has attempted to reestablish diplomatic relations with the island nation after a hiatus of more than fifty years. The impact of American tourism for Cuba and for the entire Caribbean region could be profound, but Congress so far seems hostile to rapprochement. Cuba is indeed the land down under us and is only 90 miles from Key West, Florida.

Cuba is the largest island in the Greater Antilles (and thus in the Caribbean) and its history has long been entwined with the United States. At one point, Cuba was a possession of the US, but even after it became "independent," the US reserved the right to intervene in Cuban affairs whenever the US thought it necessary.

*Columbus discovered Cuba on his first voyage to the New World. According to most sources, he named the island "Juana" after an heir to the Spanish throne.* Some European maps subsequently labeled the island as 'Cinpangu," a term Europeans used for Japan at the time.

> Dr. G. says: Although there is some evidence that suggests Columbus thought he was in Japan, I am skeptical. While longitude was not measured accurately from shipboard at the time, latitude was. Japan's latitude was known, and it, of course, differs substantially from Cuba's.

\* \* \*

Cuba as a whole was not a particularly important part of New Spain, Spain's colonial possessions. There was no gold and none of the spices that Columbus and later explorers continued to seek. Havana, due to its harbor, however, was highly important; it became a base for the exploration of Mexico. It eventually became the third largest city in the New World in the eighteenth century (after Mexico City and Lima). Meanwhile, the rest of Cuba remained lightly populated.

During the Seven Years' War (1756–1763), Great Britain invaded Cuba and took possession of it. Trade relations were established with Britain's North American colonies. African slaves were imported in considerable numbers and sugar plantations were expanded. *At the conclusion of the war, however, Britain returned Cuba to Spanish rule in exchange for Florida.*

\* \* \*

During the first two decades of the nineteenth century, Spain lost most of its colonies in North America. Wars of liberation raged in South America and in Mexico. Cuba, however, remained loyal to Spain, perhaps not so much because the sentiments of the average

Cuba

Cuban were pro-Spanish, but because Spanish military power was well established in Cuba. Independence movements waxed and waned in Cuba during the remainder of the nineteenth century. By the 1890s, the Spanish had built concentration camps (perhaps the world's first) in Cuba in which to place those suspected of activities in favor of independence. The conditions in these camps were scandalous, and tens of thousands died of disease and starvation, or at least this was reported in the New York newspapers. The United States sent the battleship *Maine* to Havana Harbor, allegedly to protect American citizens and interests. *A large explosion occurred on the* Maine *on February 15, 1898, and she sunk in Havana Harbor;* three-quarters of her crew perished. Although the cause of the explosion has never been determined, the American press blamed Spain, and the battle cry, "Remember the Maine," eventually led to the Spanish American War.

Dr. G. says: Although the United States has fought a number of wars, only five, including the Spanish-American War, were declared by Congress. While the distinction between a declared and undeclared war may seem unimportant, the only crime defined in the US Constitution is treason, and that crime can only occur in a time of war (presumably, a declared war).

\* \* \*

The American war with Spain was short-lived. The United States declared war in April 1898, and the fighting stopped in August of the same year. As a result of the peace treaty ending the war, the US acquired Cuba, Puerto Rico, the Philippines, and Guam. At the time Congress declared war, it also passed the Teller Amendment which prohibited the United States from annexing Cuba. US occupation of Cuba was therefore short, but two related medical discoveries by US doctors there were highly important (and probably enabled the construction of the Panama Canal). Dr. Walter Reed proved that yellow fever was transmitted by the mosquito, and Dr. William Gorgas rid Cuba of yellow fever and malaria by mosquito control methods.

Fulgencio Batista was elected president of Cuba from 1940 until 1944. He wanted to be president again in 1952, but it was apparent that he would not get the needed votes. What an election could not accomplish, a coup could. *Batista was Cuba's dictator from 1952 until 1959. A revolution overthrew him in 1959, and Fidel Castro emerged as the new leader of Cuba.* Castro's political views were suspected, but unknown. In 1961, *an invasion, orchestrated by the CIA, featured bombing of three airfields and a sea-borne landing at the Bay of Pigs.* Castro's forces defeated the invading force in three days, at which point Fidel proclaimed himself to be a Marxist-Leninist. Castro's victory was a huge defeat for US interests throughout the Latin Americas.

> Dr. G. says: The tiny size of the invasion force (about 1,400 troops) clearly implies that major support was expected from anti-Castro forces inside Cuba. Castro took strong measures against real and potential internal enemies; he imprisoned or otherwise detained thousands.

\*    \*    \*

One of Castro's leading lieutenants, an Argentinian by birth, Che Guevara, became a folk hero throughout Latin America. Castro and Guevara drifted apart ideologically, with Guevara favoring the communism of Mao Tse-Tung's China, and Castro favoring the Soviet Union (and the financial aid it brought to Cuba). Che left Cuba, apparently to foment revolution in other countries. *He was killed in Bolivia, thus following in the footsteps of Butch Cassidy and the Sundance Kid who also were killed there.*

# *From Geography . . .*

## *to Gastronomy . . .*

~

Food for Thought:

*On New Year's Eve, at the stroke of midnight, twelve grapes are often eaten (to remember each month) and cider is served.*

—Cuban tradition

~

## *Recipe for:*

Arroz con Pollo

# ARROZ CON POLLO

The first time I made this dish, I was a young married woman and loved that this recipe used beer in it. I will always use a local beer (and you should, too), the darker the better for a more malty flavor. This may look like a complicated, many-ingredient, lots of chopping kind of recipe, but believe me, it is worth the effort, and you can double the recipe for a larger crowd if needed.

I spoke with my friend Sonia Martinez, who grew up in Cuba, to ask what makes this authentically Cuban, and she explained that it is the unique combinations of flavors that meld Spanish, African, and Caribbean spices and produce. Cubans also have a wonderful sense of family, and she shared many wonderful memories of her youth living there. Sonia has an arroz con pollo recipe on her website, soniatasteshawaii.com, and I combined some of her recipe with my own to create a new variation on this traditional dish.

I added vanilla to allow another depth to this, making it one of my favorite meals to showcase vanilla in. You can choose to use whatever cut of chicken you like, but I always enjoy the darker meat of the thigh or an airline cut—with lots of skin to go with it. Just make sure you drain out extra fat that is rendered often—you don't want to start a grease fire! The leftovers are even better the next day since the flavors get to absorb even more—plus, when you heat it up in a skillet, the rice gets a nice crust that makes for a palatable experience—a poached egg with the leftover rice makes a perfect breakfast.

## INGREDIENTS

8 skin-on, bone-in chicken thighs

½ tablespoon ground oregano

½ tablespoon ground cumin

½ tablespoon pimenton (smoked paprika)

3 tablespoons EVOO

3 tablespoons fresh orange juice

Salt and pepper

1 lb. chorizo (I use a Portuguese sausage, Mo'ono brand)

1 medium onion, finely chopped

1 medium red bell pepper, seeded and finely chopped

1 orange bell pepper, seeded and finely chopped

4 garlic cloves, minced

1 14 oz. can chopped, organic tomatoes (or two medium fresh)

3 tablespoons capers, rinsed and drained

1 bottle of local beer, stout or porter (I used Maui Brewing Co.'s Coconut Porter)

3 cups chicken or vegetable broth

2 teaspoons vanilla extract

¼ teaspoon saffron threads

Kosher salt and ground pepper to taste

4 cups Arborio rice

2 cups frozen petit pois, thawed

1 cup Marcona almonds, chopped and lightly toasted

## MY METHOD

Make a paste with the spices, olive oil, and orange juice. Slather the chicken with the paste and marinate for at least an hour and up to four. Remove from marinade and scrape off excess, reserving it for later. and sprinkle liberally with salt and pepper.

In a medium pot, heat chicken broth, vanilla, and saffron. Bring to a simmer and turn off.

Heat heavy-bottomed stockpot to high heat and, in batches, flash sear chicken on all sides until browned, about 2–3 minutes per side, using tongs to get the sides browned and draining excess fat as needed. Remove and place on a plate. Drain out fat and carefully wipe out pot with a paper towel.

In the same pot, cook sausage until browned and fat is rendered. Using a slotted spoon, remove from pan onto a paper towel–lined plate. Pour off excess fat.

Turn heat to medium. Add reserved marinade. Add in onion and peppers and cook until soft, about 8 minutes. Add in garlic and stir for another minute. Add in tomatoes and capers.

Return the chicken to the pot. Add in the beer. Increase heat and cook for 2 minutes.

Add in rice and chicken broth mixture. Bring to a boil, cover, and reduce heat. Cook until the rice has absorbed the liquid, about 30–35 minutes, stirring in the petit pois in the last 5 minutes of cooking. If the rice is still *al dente*, add in some water (or more broth), cover and continue to cook on very low heat. If the rice has too much liquid, cook uncovered for 10–15 minutes until the liquid is reduced.

Serve on a large platter and sprinkle with the toasted almonds. Enjoy!

*Arroz con pollo (photo by bbf)*

# CHAPTER
# 18

# EXTINCTIONS

*Question 111: What important food resource did John Cabot give to the British that became virtually extinct in the 1990s?*

*Question 112: What species was eradicated from the island of Mauritius, giving rise to an expression concerning mortality?*

*Question 113: Martha was the last of her kind and died in the Cincinnati Zoo, but her species was once the most abundant bird in North America and perhaps the world. What kind of bird was she?*

*Question 114: What large mammal, once ranging widely over Asia and Europe, became extinct when the last one died in 1627 in Poland?*

*Question 115: Which whale species has become extinct in modern times?*

*Question 116: How do you make Tatonka Tourtiere and Bacalao a Gomes de Sa?*

Nothing attracts students to the ecological branch of geography like extinctions! Whales, coral reefs, newts, and salamanders, threatened with annihilation, stir the passions of throngs of young students. At times, it seemed to me that the demise of Bambi's mom was behind all this. Unfortunately, passion is not a substitute for knowledge. Few students seem willing to undertake the heavy lifting that is necessary to understand the process of extinction and, especially, the genetics that's behind much of it.

Nothing annoys passionate students of this ilk more than the suggestion that species extinction is the fate of almost all species—more

Dr. G. says: Sometimes we think a species has become extinct, usually because we haven't seen it in decades or centuries, and then it pops up again. Such species are known as Lazarus taxa, and none is more astounding than the coelacanth caught off the coast of South Africa in 1938. This species of fish was believed to have become extinct 65 million years ago! We seem to be doing our best to correct this error since fishermen in the Comoros Islands catch about a dozen a year from a total population in the low hundreds at most.

than 99.9 percent in fact. Humans had little to do with most extinctions because we weren't around until very recently. Nevertheless, we **have** caused a number of species to vanish before their time.

Among the most dramatic extinction or near-extinction situations in recent times involves the depletion of ocean fisheries. Shortly after Columbus came to the New World, *John Cabot gave England its first colony, Newfoundland. Now, Newfoundland did not offer the most agreeable environment that one might want in a colony, but it offered an incredible offshore resource: the Atlantic cod.* Other Europeans (especially the Basque) may have been fishing Newfoundland's Grand Banks before Cabot got there, but the stories that Cabot's men brought back to Bristol fueled an exploitation of the Newfoundland cod fishery that lasted for centuries. The Grand Banks fed millions of people. In 1992, Canada closed the Grand Banks to commercial fishing because the cod population had collapsed. After more than twenty years, the cod have not come back in commercial quantities.

\*   \*   \*

Situations similar to the fishery collapse in Newfoundland have occurred elsewhere: for example, the anchovy collapse in Peru and the herring collapse in Northern Iceland. One informed estimate is that 70 percent of the world's fisheries have collapsed. As far as we know, these population collapses are due entirely to overfishing and, while there are indeed other fish in the sea, unless certain fishing practices are curtailed, especially bottom trawling, which destroys habitat, commercial fishing could destroy the resource upon which it depends.

Some species exist in small ecological niches and may have adapted to their habitats by low reproduction rates in the face of a lack of predators that otherwise would control their populations. In such a case, even relatively modest changes in their environment could lead to rapid extinction. Hawaii, for example, has dozens of bird species already extinct or highly endangered due to both introduced predators and loss of habitat. The most famous example, however, is *the dodo, a flightless bird found on Mauritius in the Indian Ocean. Escaped slaves are said to have ravaged the population and the dodo became extinct without much notice at the time. "Dead as a dodo," however, became an expression in our language.*

Mauritius shared another extinct species with its Indian Ocean neighbor, Reunion. In the eighteenth century and earlier, the small Mauritian flying fox was abundant and widespread. The only written account of this species of bat comes from a document written in 1772. One hundred years later, it was extinct on both islands.

*Painting of a dodo (by Cornelis Saftleven, 1638. Housed at the Boijmans Museum in Rotterdam)*

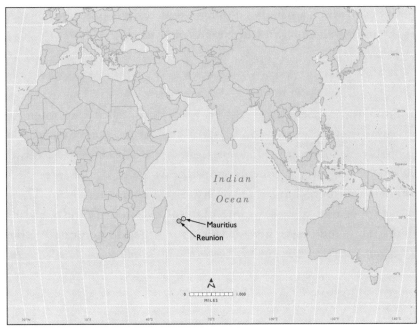

*Mauritius and Reunion, Indian Ocean*

\*   \*   \*

We are astounded when we learn that 60 million bison were slaughtered on the Great Plains in the years after the Civil War, but, of course, the species did survive and is now being raised commercially. The fate of the passenger pigeon, however, may be the most remarkable extinction story in modern times. The passenger pigeon was incredibly abundant and wide-ranging in North America; it was the most common bird on the continent, and some authorities think, the most abundant of all bird species in the world. As late as the 1860s, flocks of billions were seen. *In 1914, the last passenger pigeon, Martha, died at the Cincinnati Zoo.*

The impact of the extinction of the passenger pigeon was always made real to me because my father, as a boy, recalled seeing flocks of the birds in the wetlands that surrounded his house. Forty years later, in the same swamp, I witnessed an immense flock of redwing blackbirds, which are believed to have replaced the passenger pigeon as the most abundant bird in North America.

*  *  *

Sometimes species can exist in protected niches even when we presume they are extinct. So it is with the auroch, an animal that is probably the forebear of all domesticated cattle. It was generally considered a prehistoric animal; indeed, cave paintings portray these animals that were hunted in prehistoric Europe and Asia. There were two separate domestications of the animal—one in India leading to the zebu, and one in Eurasia leading to other domesticated cattle. *The auroch actually survived until 1627, when the last died in a remote forest in Poland.*

*  *  *

Americans are concerned about the fate of the whales; you could tell that when one of the *Star Trek* movies was devoted to the topic. Not everyone worldwide shares that concern. The Japanese eat them, and I saw bumper stickers in Iceland with a picture of a whale and the words: "Kill them all." (Neither nation subscribes fully to the moratorium on whale harvesting.)

Despite the best efforts of Japan, Russia, Iceland, and Norway, whale populations appear to be stabilizing and even increasing. *Only one whale species has become extinct in modern times: the Atlantic gray whale.*

Dr. G. says: Hundreds of Pacific humpback whales visit Hawaii in the winter to bear their young. They are particularly common along the south shores of the major islands. About once a week, a whale will be spotted caught in fishing gear, often in nets and flotation devices that prevent it from diving. I have seen huge piles of debris from fishing fleets on island shores. My conclusion is that whaling is not the biggest enemy of whales—factory fishing fleets are.

# *From Geography . . .*

# *. . . to Gastronomy*

~

### Food for Thought:

*"If all the beasts were gone, we would die from great loneliness of spirit. For whatever happens to the beast, happens to us. All things are connected."*

—Chief Seattle

~

## *Recipe for:*

Tatonka Tourtiere
Bacalao
Bacalao a Gomes de Sa

# TATONKA TOURTIERE

*Serves 6–8*

My husband's uncle in Alberta had a buffalo ranch, and we were lucky enough to visit. We had buffalo burgers for dinner that cold wintry night and played Trivial Pursuit! Here is a delicious pie using protein rich, lean buffalo, alongside pork and rich spices. This requires a double crust pastry—one for both the top and bottom, so use your favorite recipe, or the ones in the refrigerated section of your grocery store will work just fine. This recipe will make more than enough filling for one pie, so if you make additional pastry, you can make smaller hand pies (or tartlets), or place the mixture in ovenproof ramekins and top with the pastry for a lighter meal.

## INGREDIENTS

4 tablespoons butter
1 large onion, finely chopped
½ cup carrots, finely chopped
3 celery stalks, finely chopped
2 parsnips, chopped
4 garlic cloves, minced
1 teaspoon fennel seeds
½ teaspoon cloves
½ teaspoon allspice
½ teaspoon cinnamon
½ teaspoon cardamom
1 tablespoon vanilla extract
1 large tomato, chopped
2 tablespoons tomato paste
1½ lb. ground bison
1½ lb. ground pork
Salt and pepper to taste
Double short crust dough
Sour cream for serving

## MY METHOD

In a large, heavy-bottomed pot, melt butter over medium heat. Add in onions, carrots, celery, and parsnips. Sauté 8–10 minutes, until soft. Add in garlic and cook for one more minute, stirring. Add in all spices and vanilla. Stir and continue to cook for 2–3 minutes. Add in tomato and tomato paste, stir and cook for 2–3 minutes. Raise heat to medium-high and add in bison and pork. Cook until all the meat is browned, and most of the liquid is absorbed, about 30 minutes. Line a large bowl with 4 paper towels and pour mixture in to drain any remaining liquid. Allow to cool.

Fill the bottom and sides of a 10-inch pie plate with one of the pastry dough. Press it in and crimp the edges. Fill the pie with the meat filling, mounding it slightly. Take your second piece of pastry and drape it over the top, crimping the edges together to seal the pie. Make steam vents in the center of the dough by using a sharp paring knife and making 3 slits about 1-inch long.

Bake at 375°F for one hour. Allow to cool for at least 20 minutes before slicing. Serve with sour cream.

*Tatonka tourtiere (photo by T. M. Reddekopp)*

# BACALAO, SALTED COD

Salted cod is a dish that is traditional in many cultures. Here in Hawaii, it is used by Portuguese families and is readily available at any supermarket. Years ago, I had a themed dinner around Portuguese food and decided to try my hand at making my own salted cod. I was fearful it would be too salty, but if you soak it properly, it truly is so tender, moist, and delectable. While very easy to make, it does require advanced preparation, so plan accordingly.

## INGREDIENTS

**Cod fillet, skinned, deboned, and rinsed**
**Kosher salt, enough to encase the fillets**

## MY METHOD

In a shallow container, pour a layer of salt. Lay the fillets on top of the salt and cover the fish with more salt, making sure you encase it completely. Refrigerate for 48 hours.

Remove fillets from salt and rinse. Pat dry with paper towels, and press very gently to expel excess moisture.

You may choose now to preserve it for storage or soak it to use the next day. You will need to soak it for 24 hours, changing the water every 6–8 hours, before using it in the following recipe. On the last soaking, place the fillets in a large, heavy-bottomed skillet. Fill with water and heat until simmering. Turn off heat and allow the fillets to cool. Drain and pat dry. The salted cod is now ready to be used.

If you would like to preserve it for future use, wrap it in parchment paper and place it in your refrigerator for a week or until it is completely dried. Wrap tightly in plastic wrap and freeze for up to 6 months. When you are ready to use this bacalao, you will need to defrost and follow the same soaking before use as written above.

# BACALAO A GOMES DE SA

*Serves 4–6*

This is a wonderfully filling, make-ahead meal for any time of the day. Traditionally, it does not include sausage, but I like the smoky richness that just a little will bring to this dish.

## INGREDIENTS

2 lbs. bacalao, soaked, rinsed, patted dry and flaked into bite-sized pieces

2½ lbs. red potatoes, cut into ½-inch chunks (or whatever size you like to eat)

½ cup EVOO

½ lb. Portuguese sausage, chopped small

2 large onions, sliced

4 garlic cloves, minced

1 teaspoon ground oregano

Salt and pepper to taste

2 large tomatoes, chopped (or one 14 oz. can of diced tomatoes, drained)

6 hardboiled eggs, peeled and sliced

1 14oz. can black olives, drained and roughly chopped

Garlic chives, for garnish

## MY METHOD

Cook potatoes in water until tender (the skins will just start to pull away from the flesh of the potato) but not mushy. Drain and set aside.

In a heavy-bottomed skillet, cook sausage on medium heat until browned and fat is rendered. Remove from pan with a slotted spoon onto a plate lined with a paper towel to absorb excess grease. Pour off fat from pan. Add in ¼ cup oil. Return heat to medium and add onions, cooking until tender, 5–7 minutes. Add in garlic, stirring, and cook for one more minute. Add oregano. Add tomatoes and cook until heated through. Season with salt and pepper.

In a large casserole, begin layering by adding first half of the potatoes, then half of the salted cod, then half of the sausage, then half of the onion mixture, then half of the olives. Make a second layer. Drizzle all the oil from the pan over the top and the additional ¼ cup of olive oil.

Bake at 350°F for 45 minutes, or until the potatoes are golden. Garnish with the sliced eggs and chives. Serve hot, warm, or at room temperature with some hot sauce.

# GOLD RUSHES

Geographers and others who teach in universities undergo periodic review of their performance. For some reason, those in charge always ask about one's "teaching philosophy." Of course, no one doing the reviewing had the slightest idea about what a teaching philosophy is or what it ought to be. Nevertheless, they never liked mine, so I changed it each time I was reviewed. As time went by, they liked it less and less. One of my last efforts was a quote from Mark Twain, "Everything has its limit . . . iron ore cannot be educated into gold." This was deemed terribly politically incorrect by the higher university authority, but it does introduce this chapter.

Are gold rushes over? Probably. It is not the lack of potential gold that limits the possibility but rather restrictions on international migration—and sometimes on movement inside a country. National lotteries and casinos seem to satisfy the same urges as gold rushes—and in considerably greater comfort. Of course, things other than gold can

Selected Gold Rushes

California

Sacramento
San Francisco

Dahlonega Mint · Charlotte Mint

Appalachian

Tierra del Fuego

Witwatersrand

New South Wales

N

0 [_____] 2,000
MILES

Gold rushes

glitter as well. Jobs on the Alaska Pipeline probably had more influence on Alaska than the gold rush at Nome, and, by golly, fracking in North Dakota has taken on gold rush proportions, you betcha.

Gold rushes have been studied sufficiently, so we understand that they go through production stages, beginning with placer mining (basically, recovering high quality gold-bearing ore on the surface) and extending to sluice boxes, high-pressure hoses, and underground mining. Geographers, however, have not so much studied gold rushes as they have studied their mirror image: natural disasters. People rush to gold and rush away from natural disasters like earthquakes and volcanic eruptions.

Mathematicians have formulated a theory that explains why predictions don't always work out. Chaos theory explains why, even when we know that one thing determines another, we still cannot always predict the exact outcome. Extending this idea outside pure mathematics is a bit of a stretch, but some have tried. Geographers, for example, can reasonably say that the number of people traveling between city A and city B is determined by the product of the population of A and B and diminished by the distance between them. Certain determinants, however, that we didn't measure accurately when we thought about people moving from A to B and from B to A can introduce real chaos in our attempt to predict. Gold rushes and natural disasters are examples. If gold is discovered in A, people will rush there, in numbers all out of proportion to what we expected. Or a volcanic eruption at B will cause people to flee, far beyond what we might have predicted as "normal" movement.

Dr. G. says: Personally, I have never thought that human behavior can be "determined," or perhaps stated with less emphasis, that we can actually identify or measure all those things that might determine human behavior. Chaos theory works mathematically because one part of an equation can determine another part. It works less well in the social sciences.

The parallel (or mirror image) between disasters and gold rushes includes the fact that information about the events becomes distorted with the distance away from the occurrence. Case studies (including one personal experience) reveal that information distortion can be any which way. Often, the amount of gold found and the severity of the disaster are exaggerated to Herculean proportions, but there are times when a significant gold find or a disaster is ignored or underreported. Concerning disasters, the international press seems fixated on the "death count," but a natural disaster can have horrifying and lethal long-term effects, with few immediate casualties.

Probably the most important geographic effect of a gold rush is the redistribution of population. Just as we would expect, gold is not discovered lining the sidewalks of New York, but in remote places where few have gone before. San Francisco, for example, had a population of around 200 before the gold rush, and while its growth and present size can be attributed to a number of factors over the years, there is no question that the forty-niners laid the foundation for that growth (the miners, not the football team).

*The first gold rush in the United States—and one of the first anywhere—occurred in North Carolina at the turn of the nineteenth century.* It began soon after gold was discovered on the Reed farm in Cabarrus County. John Reed eventually mined gold underground and became rich in the process. A few years later, gold was discovered in Lumpkin County, Georgia (northeast of Atlanta). By the time of the Civil War, the Appalachian gold belt had been extended north as far as Virginia and southwest into Alabama.

While white settlers flocked to the gold belt, a great deal of the land where gold actually was—or thought to be—was owned by the so-called Five Civilized Tribes, especially the Cherokee. When I use the word "owned" here, I mean a formal treaty had been signed between the US government and the Cherokee Nation. Moreover, some land was owned by Cherokees who had purchased it from white owners. My college history texts do mention the expulsion of these southern tribes to the Oklahoma Territory (The Trail of Tears) but the forced removal is invariably accounted for by the desire of planters to obtain prime land for cotton—the gold rush is hardly mentioned, yet it must have been an important factor.

It is difficult to determine how much gold came from the Appalachian gold belt, but we do know that thousands of ounces of gold were sent to the US Mint in Philadelphia, and, far more significantly, that branch mints were opened in Dahlonega, Georgia, and Charlotte, North Carolina. Perhaps you have not heard of Dahlonega, since today it is a village-sized place with a population of around 5,000. In the height of the gold rush, however, Dahlonega was said to have had over 15,000 miners in addition to others who provided goods and services to the gold-seekers.

The California gold rush was perhaps the most significant gold rush of them all. While the amount of gold discovered was substantial, the real prize was California itself. The presence of gold filled California with Americans who overthrew Mexican rule and relatively quickly brought California into the Union. California was then connected by rail with the rest of the country in 1869, only twenty-one years after the gold rush began. An estimated 300,000 people moved to California between 1850 and 1855.

California proved to be the gold prospector's dream, at least initially. Gold nuggets could simply be picked up from the ground. In the absence of any legal restrictions on mining, California was virtually lawless. For example, gold was discovered on John Sutter's farm and ranch on the American River. His land was overrun with squatters who stole his crops and killed his cattle. Sutter was ruined by the gold rush.

Dr. G. says: Government restrictions were already in place at the time of the New South Wales rush and at the Klondike.

One would not expect a culinary tradition to emerge from a gold rush, but one did in California. French bakers arrived in San Francisco and introduced the ancient technique of making bread from a sourdough batter. Sourdough bread is a symbol of San Francisco and is embodied in "Sourdough Sam," the mascot of the 49ers football team. Sourdough was carried into Alaska and the Klondike during the gold rush there. A "sourdough" in Alaska was a prospector who had kept his starter dough alive for a winter (some say a true sourdough must accomplish this feat north of the Arctic Circle).

\* \* \*

Gold rushes continued through the nineteenth and into the early twentieth century. A big strike was discovered in the Rocky Mountains, especially at and near Pikes Peak. "Pikes Peak or Bust" became a motto of the gold seekers. *Today, of course, Pikes Peak is in Colorado, but when gold was discovered in 1859, it was part of the Kansas Territory.*

*Pikes Peak (photo by "Hogs555")*

\*    \*    \*

Finding nuggets of gold just lying around sounded promising to the forty-niners, but it did not work out well for Edward Hargraves, an Australian who returned home with no gold but with an idea: the hills in California where gold had been found reminded him of hills in New South Wales. Hargraves found gold there and started the Australian gold rush. Government officials had known about Australian gold for some time, but had suppressed knowledge of it. *In 1872, the largest gold nugget ever found was discovered in New South Wales by Bernhardt Holtermann: it weighed over 700 pounds!*

\*    \*    \*

The greatest gold strike of all time was made in South Africa—the Witwatersrand region. It is responsible for the city of Johannesburg and for probably the majority of all gold taken from the earth. Unlike California and New South Wales, there were not huge nuggets to be found but rather rich veins of gold that could be mined underground—and which are still being mined today. It is tempting to think that the discovery of gold there was the southernmost gold rush—but it wasn't.

*The southernmost gold rush began in 1883 and lasted until 1906. It was occasioned by the grounding of the French ship* Artique *at Tierra del Fuego, at the southern tip of South America.* Members of a rescue party discovered gold and, as usual, miners poured in from around the world. Punta Arenas became a substantial city in the area. A commercial operation brought in miners from Dalmatia to add to the mix of nationalities attempting to find gold.

> Dr. G. says: It is not certain who spotted the Dalmatians at Tierra del Fuego.

\*    \*    \*

Buffalo, New York, is famous for O. J. Simpson and . . . and
. . . and . . . (what else?) . . . Fran Striker! Striker wrote the *Lone
Ranger* books and radio scripts. He also wrote the scripts for Sergeant
Preston of the Royal Canadian Mounted Police. "On King, on you
huskies" never became as popular as "Hi ho Silver," but it served
the same purpose. Sergeant Preston was always mushing between
Whitehorse and Dawson, but exactly where these places were was a
bit obscure. The great Klondike gold rush fooled a lot of Americans
because those rushing seemed to be going to Alaska. Indeed, over
100,000 people went to the Klondike gold fields between 1896 and
1899—and almost all of them got there by first going to Skagway,
Alaska, then crossing to Canada's Yukon Territory by a very difficult
uphill route. While there were substantial gold discoveries in Alaska,
*the Klondike is in Canada.*

*Skagway, Alaska (photo by bbf)*

# From Geography . . .

## . . . to Gastronomy

~

### Food for Thought:

*You can't be sad while enjoying a cinnamon roll (with lots of extra frosting).*

—T. M. Reddekopp

~

**Recipe for:**

Rachel's Cinnamon Twists

# RACHEL'S CINNAMON TWISTS

A few years ago, we welcomed some of the sales staff of Hawaiian Airlines to our place for a luncheon and tour. It afforded us an opportunity to take our very first family vacation (where it was not tacked on to Jim working)—and we were going to The Mainland! It was a big trip for all seven of us—it was a privilege to get to see some of the most beautiful scenery. It did take my breath away at the Grand Canyon. Words simply cannot express the feeling of wonder and awe I felt there. I took a photo of my kids, sitting on the southern rim with the sun setting behind them. The temperature was dipping and on our tailgate we nibbled bread, cheese, salami, and olives.

We also got to do our very first road trip (there are not enough miles in Hawaii to make a road trip). We visited with our friends, Chris and Rachel Cox in an old mining town in Crystal, Colorado. Their family owns the mill, and it is one of the most photographed sites in the area—and difficult to come by. You have to have a four-wheel drive vehicle, and it is a sheer drop down with no guardrail, just boulders and lots of smaller shifting rocks. People have died on the road.

Everything has to be brought in—except for the trout that you catch in the stream. We caught a lot; had many bonfires, hikes, cookouts, storytelling, outhouse using; and learned how to cook on a wood burning stove. Rachel has been cooking on a wood burning stove for more than 25 years and has made these so many times she has lost count (I asked!). These I crave, and I have been known to beg my daughter to make them. She likes to make them for me with lots of cream cheese frosting (bless her!).

*Makes 16*

## INGREDIENTS FOR DOUGH

3½ cups flour

¼ cup sugar

½ teaspoon salt

2¼ teaspoons yeast

½ cup (softened) + 2 tablespoons (melted) butter, divided

1 egg beaten

1 cup whole milk

1 tablespoon vanilla extract

## INGREDIENTS FOR FILLING

1 tablespoon vanilla extract

⅓ cup finely chopped macadamia nuts or walnuts (optional)

1 tablespoon cinnamon

½ cup butter

½ cup brown sugar

## INGREDIENTS FOR FROSTING

4 oz. cream cheese, softened to room temperature

1 cup powdered sugar

¼ cup butter, softened to room temperature

1 teaspoon vanilla extract

1–2 tablespoons heavy cream or whole milk (add more if you
want a thinner consistency)

## MY METHOD FOR THE DOUGH

Mix flour, salt, and yeast in a large bowl. Heat milk in a small pot
and add butter to melt. Turn off heat and allow to cool. When the
milk is cooled, stir in sugar, egg, and vanilla. Combine with flour
mixture and gently mix until dough comes together. Knead gently
in the bowl for 3–5 minutes until it is soft, pliable, and springs back
when lightly pressed.

Cover bowl with a dish towel and allow the dough to rest for 20 minutes.

While you are waiting, make the filling, melt the 2 tablespoons of butter, and make the frosting. (Directions follow below)

When your 20 minutes are up, separate the dough into 3 equal parts, and on a lightly floured surface, roll out into 3, 9-inch circles.

Place one round on a rimmed sheet pan lined with parchment and then brush with butter. Sprinkle on ⅓ of the prepared filling. Repeat with the other two rounds.

Leaving about a 2-inch diameter circle intact in the center of the dough rounds, use a sharp paring knife and radiate cuts toward the outer edge of rounds, cutting 16 slices (this works wonderfully if you look at it like a clock and cut it into quarters, and then each quarter into two, then each of those pieces into two).

Lift up each wedge and holding it in place, twist gently 3 or 4 times, replacing the edge where it began, pressing it gently but firmly into place.

*Rachel's cinnamon twists (photo by T. M. Reddekopp)*

Allow to rest for 20 minutes in a warm place.

Bake at 350°F for 20 minutes. Cool in the pan on a rack for 10–15 minutes.

Drizzle or spread with the cream cheese frosting while the twists are still warm.

## MY METHOD FOR THE FILLING

Using a rubber spatula, cream all ingredients together until smooth.

## MY METHOD FOR THE FROSTING

Stir first four ingredients together until creamy. Continue stirring and add cream or milk until desired thickness is achieved.

# RIVERS AND CIVILIZATIONS

*Question 123: What river is associated with the Harappan civilization?*

*Question 124: At the mouth of what river does one find Marsh Arabs?*

*Question 125: According to Herodotus, what is the gift of the Nile?*

*Question 126: What is the "road to Mandalay"?*

*Question 127: What are the two rivers that meet in Pittsburgh and what river do they form?*

*Question 128: How do you make North African Pan-Fried Bread?*

Occasionally, university professors are asked difficult questions by their students. Why, for example (I was once asked) did the Egyptians build a great civilization over a few thousand years, whereas the Australian aborigines, with more than 30,000 years to work, did not even develop agriculture? One of my professors (with a strong in-

> Dr. G. says: Some years ago it became common for professors to be "evaluated" by their students. The format is usually a questionnaire containing mostly inane questions that have little to do with real learning or teaching. What actually should happen is that a professor should be periodically required to answer questions from his students while a committee of the professor's peers are present.

clination for economic rationale) argued that for a society to advance, it had to first develop a food surplus, thus freeing some from a constant quest for food and water. This point has merit, but it is an inadequate answer for a geographer. Before people can develop a food surplus, they need something to work with. Some (shallow-thinking) geographers looked to early civilizations and noticed that rivers were central to these developments; rivers were thus said to be the cause: a source of fresh water, a place to find food, a place allowing transport, a renewal of fertile soil at flood stage, and so on. The problem with this argument is (among other things) that Australia has some really nice rivers—it could do with more, I know. A river is not enough: riverine civilizations that developed needed plants and animals that could be domesticated, thus increasing the food supply. What has been (or can be) domesticated among the native flora and fauna of Australia? Something needed to come in from outside before Australia's rivers could create a civilization—pretty much what actually happened. In brief, a river is nice, but won't suffice.

Geographers and historians have done a great job in lettings us know about the great riverine civilizations in Egypt and Mesopotamia; probably the reason for this is that both are mentioned in the Judeo-Christian handbook, the Bible. We have also been somewhat informed about China's Yellow River civilization. *The Harappan civilization, however, does not ring a mental bell with us even when it's paired with its principal river, the Indus.* The surprising thing about this is that the Indus civilization likely covered more area and included more people than the civilizations found in Egypt and Mesopotamia. We know much less about the Harappan civilization, whose remnants are mostly found in modern Pakistan; serious archeological work in the Indus Valley didn't begin until the 1930s, and many of the remains had been destroyed or seriously disturbed before any scientific work began. Contributing to this situation was the reality that many of the Indus tributaries along which the Harappan civilization developed have dried up.

\*    \*    \*

Were there weapons of mass destruction in Iraq before US and coalition forces invaded? Should Saddam Hussein have been overthrown? Answer those for homework, but before you answer the second, do you know what Saddam was doing *to the delta of the Tigris-Euphrates?* This river system, rising in Turkey, sustained the civilizations that developed between the two rivers (literally "meso potamia"). At the point where the rivers drain into the Persian Gulf, there is substantial marsh land in the delta. Saddam Hussein decided to drain this marsh system. His motives are not clear to me. Normally, one drains marsh lands in order to expand agricultural land. Since Saddam is no longer hanging around, we can't ask him. His critics claim, however, that his motives were entirely military: he wanted to rid the area of Shiites who lived in the area and opposed his regime. *These people, known as Marsh Arabs, destroyed dikes and dams that Saddam had built as soon as Saddam was gone.* Today, the once-rich ecosystem of the delta region has been partially restored.

\*    \*    \*

The Nile is the longest river in the world, except to some fans of the Amazon. The only issue that keeps this question of greatest length from being definitively settled is that we are still not quite sure where the source of the Nile is (despite all the British explorers with pith helmets who died trying to find it). The funny goose-foot that we find at the mouth of many rivers is called a "delta" because the Nile's looks like the Greek letter delta. The Nile's delta is over 150 miles across and has been a remarkable fertile and productive area for thousands of years.

The most significant change in the Nile in recent times was the construction of the Aswan Dam, finished in the 1960s. This was one of the most controversial projects ever undertaken. On the one hand, it destroyed or required the removal of invaluable antiquities along the shore areas of the lake created behind the dam (either Lake Aswan or Lake Nasser) and displaced over 100,000 people; on the other hand, it controlled the periodic flooding or droughts that destroyed agriculture downstream. Aswan has always reminded me of Hoover Dam in the United States, not only for the similar flood control that was a major objective but also because of the electrical power produced by both dams.

Is the Aswan Dam a good or bad thing? While you are deciding, remember Fuller's First Geographic Law: Nature Abhors a Lake. Since most dams produce lakes behind them, nature will be doing its best to destroy them. It costs a lot to combat nature, mostly in the dredging of the artificial lakes to remove the load of material carried downstream and dumped behind the dam.

*The question posed at the beginning of the chapter, Herodotus's famous quote about the "gift of the Nile" has been a favorite of quiz shows and trivia games for years. I have heard answers given by participants ranging from the literal "water" to the absurd "piranha." The answer is "Egypt."*

\* \* \*

Ray Bradbury's *Fahrenheit 451* became required reading for many students in high school English classes sometime after the movie of the same name came out. Book-burning was the theme of both the movie and the book. The "banned book list" (sort of like a burning, but at a lower temperature) also became the rage. A recent conversation with a high school student revealed that she knew far more books that had been banned than she had ever read. The irony of this, at least to me, is that English teachers and professors, while expressing outrage over book banning, seem to have (effectively) burned a lot of books themselves. One of the barbecued authors is Rudyard Kipling, whose stories and poems are based in British India. Tommy Atkins, Gunga Din, and Kim O'Hara are as extinct as the dinosaurs.

It is strange indeed that I would ask a question about the "Road to Mandalay" since, regardless of its virtue as poetry, the poem is really bad geography. China is not across the bay, as Kipling alleges—in fact, China is nowhere in sight. *The road to Mandalay is generally considered a reference to the Irrawaddy River, one of several rivers that contributed to the development of civilization in Southeast Asia.*

If Kipling was wrong, contemporary geographers have not done much better since we can't decide what country the Irrawaddy flows through. Many sources call the country "Myanmar," but since a junta of somewhat nasty generals insist we call it that, I prefer "Burma." Essentially, the Irrawaddy *is* Burma. It flows from north to south through the country and empties into the Andaman Sea. The generals are, aside from holding a Nobel Peace Prize winner under house arrest, building seven dams across the Irrawaddy and its tributaries.

\*    \*    \*

For much of its early history, Pittsburgh, Pennsylvania, was better connected to New Orleans than to Philadelphia. Maybe that's an overstatement, but the truth was that if westward settlers could get over the mountains of Pennsylvania, they would have crossed a more difficult east-west barrier than the Rocky Mountains. Pittsburgh sits at the point where *the Allegheny River and Monongahela River meet.* The Allegheny carries a lot of water, but it starts a few miles east of nowhere then flows north into New York before flowing south again toward Pittsburgh. As a transportation route, it's not much, but the valley through which it flows is packed with fossil fuel resources. The Monongahela had the advantage in colonial and early federal days of providing transport for settlers crossing the mountains from Virginia (or now, West Virginia) and Maryland. Still, neither river is likely to make it into the Top Ten of flowing wonders. *Once at Pittsburgh, however, they get together to form the Ohio,* and with only the falls at Louisville to get around, you can reach the Mississippi and make it all the way to New Orleans—or farther.

> Dr. G. says: Pittsburgh residents can get upset if you forget to put the h at the end (Pittsburg, Kansas, is ok, but it's Pittsburgh, Pennsylvania). In fact, however, the h in Pittsburgh was removed between 1890 and 1911.

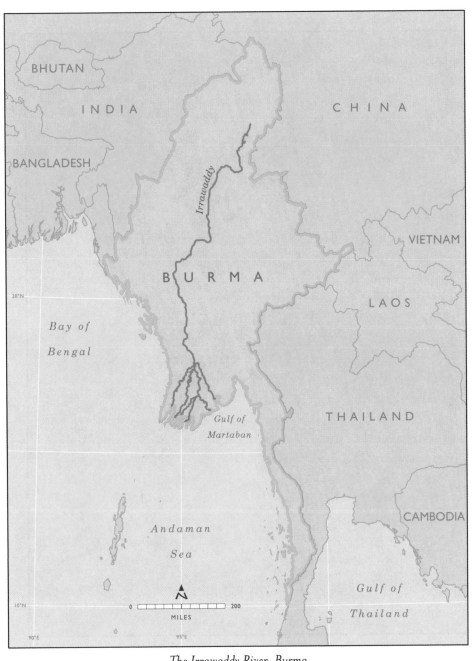

*The Irrawaddy River, Burma*

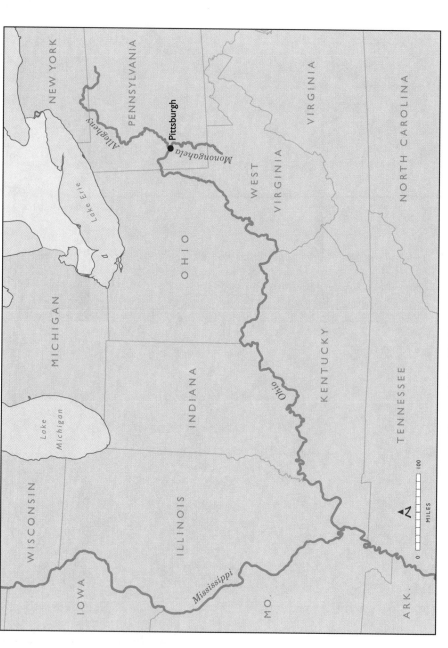

*Monongahela, Allegheny, and Ohio Rivers*

# *From Geography . . .*

*The Seine (photo by bbf)*

# *. . . to Gastronomy*

~

Food for Thought:

*"If you can't feed a hundred people, then feed just one."*

—Mother Teresa

~

**Recipe for:**

North African Pan-Fried Bread

# NORTH AFRICAN PAN-FRIED BREAD

*Makes 4 pan-sized loaves*

This was another one of those recipes where I said to my dad, "Yeah, I have lots of ancient civilization recipes on hand—let me look in my recipe box." Not! However, I was fortunate to travel with my husband on a government-sponsored trip to Morocco a few years ago, which is a country that certainly has an ancient feel to it and holds onto many of the old ways of doing things—especially in the ways of cooking.

The way that the people used a communal oven to bake their bread was intriguing—it was energy efficient, to say the least, and connected the community in a way that was new to me, and I believe it dates back to an ancient time when not everyone had the luxury of having a stove.

Each family prepared the day's bread and brought it to a wood-fired oven in the central part of the walled city of Fez. A family member would come and gather their bread later in the day. Bread was served with every meal and was always accompanied with roasted vegetables, olives, and roasted meat. This is the bread I made for a *Casablanca* inspired menu I made. It is best eaten right away, still hot and crisp from the stovetop, slathered with butter or dipped in olive oil and sprinkled with salt.

## INGREDIENTS

**3 cups flour**
**2 teaspoons instant yeast**
**I teaspoon salt**
**I cup lukewarm water**
**EVOO, about I cup**
**Chopped herbs may be added for additional flavor (optional)**

## MY METHOD

In a large bowl, combine flour, yeast, salt, and water. Stir to combine and allow to sit for a few minutes until the yeast is active and bubbles form. This dough will be very moist. If it is too moist to work with, add a bit of flour, one tablespoon at a time. If it is too dry, add water, one tablespoon at a time.

Oil your hands and lightly brush a work space with oil as well. Remove dough from the bowl and work the dough a bit, kneading gently, adding in oil to make it supple. Do not overwork it. It should be moist and still slightly sticky. With a bench scraper or knife, cut the dough into 4 portions and gently form into balls. Brush them with oil and place them on a parchment-lined baking sheet. Place them in a warm spot in your kitchen and let them rise for 30 minutes.

After 30 minutes, take one of the balls of dough and using a well-oiled rolling pin (and your hands) flatten it to about ¼-inch thickness, using additional oil as needed on your work space. Fold the flattened dough into thirds, like an envelope. Repeat this process 5 or 6 more times. On the last folding, gently stretch the dough (again using a rolling pin and your hands) into a round, about 8 inches in diameter. If the dough does not stretch easily, allow it to rest for a minute or two and then try again. It should be very pliable. Repeat this process with the remaining balls of dough. Set them aside in a warm place and allow them to rise for another 30 minutes.

After 25 minutes of the rise time, begin to heat a cast-iron skillet on medium-high (I highly recommend a cast-iron pan for this recipe—the high heat that it holds is best to fry the bread).

Take one of the rounds of dough and flatten it to a little more than ¼ inch. Brush the side you will cook first with oil and sprinkle with a little salt. Cook on the oiled side for 1 minute and then lift one side with a metal spatula to check for a nice golden brown crust. Once it is browned, brush the other side with oil, flip, and cook until browned. You can re-flip and cook again using the metal spatula to gently press the bread into the pan to brown spots that didn't cook enough.

Remove to a rack and place on a baking sheet in a warmed oven. Repeat with the remaining dough. Serve with grilled meats, the recipe for **Sweet Pepper and Onion Jam**, and/or the recipe for **Cilantro-Lime Dipping Sauce**, both found in chapter 14. Enjoy!

# THINGS CHANGE

We have had all sorts of ages and revolutionary changes in the past. After the Dark Ages came the Renaissance, then the Enlightenment, the Industrial Revolution, the Atomic Age, the Computer Age, along with many divisions within these eras. What age are we in now? I suspect that for the last fifty years or so, we have been in the Age of Change. It's not just new mechanical and electronic inventions: technological change has been rapid, but cars are still cars, and airplanes are still airplanes. Instead, it's our ideas and our behaviors that have been the real change. The incidence of marriage, for example, is less common, and, when it does occur, monogamy has been replaced by serial polygamy. The nuclear family may not get together at holidays simply because its members are separated by such great distances. World population, instead of exploding, may soon be shrinking. Americans and Europeans have changed from being religious believers to being mostly nonbeliev-ers, or so a recent survey showed.

Geography has long studied change. At one point, the emphasis in geographic research was on how one place differed from another. Essentially, an individual who traveled from one location to another experienced a change in landscape, language, religious beliefs, how people made their living, and a host of other differences. In study-ing change this way, geography was a descriptive endeavor. Later, geography became an analytic science when it examined ways that different places differed systematically and what caused or otherwise affected these differences. Later still, geography began to look at how change might occur in the future and how future change might be induced by agents or agencies. In particular, geographers became concerned with the probability of future events. Enormous future change can sometimes occur because of new ideas or things that seem insignificant at the time. The amplification of voice, for example (as I discuss below), and the subsequent application of that technology to radio waves all depended on a device called the triode invented by Lee de Forest.

Neither the Founding Fathers nor the US Constitution foresaw the development of political parties or the two-party system that has characterized American politics. The two parties that emerged in the period 1820–1850 can fairly be called the pro-Andrew Jackson Democrats and the Whigs who opposed the strong executive power that Jackson represented. Dissension within the Whig Party led to a strange situation: a sitting president, Millard Fillmore, lost the nomination of his own party for the presidency. Almost immedi-ately, a new national political party emerged. *The Republican Party was founded in Ripon, Wisconsin,* and from its onset was anti-slavery. It did not advocate the abolition of slavery but rather its containment to those states where it already existed. Republican affiliation spread like wildfire in the Northern states. In its second national conven-tion, held in Chicago in 1860, Abraham Lincoln was nominated for president in one of the great political miracles in US history.

From then until 1932, the Republican Party dominated politics in the United States. Considering that there was no Republican Party until 1854, the change it brought about was dramatic.

\*  \*  \*

The Women's Rights Movement and the Abolitionist Movement had been strongly united until after the Civil War. In 1870, the 15th Amendment to the US Constitution was ratified which granted the right to vote regardless of race—but not regardless of sex. Feminist organizations seeking suffrage became more common and more militant. Susan B. Anthony was one of the most famous of the suffragettes, particularly after her trial in Rochester, New York, in 1872 where she was convicted of—voting! At the same time that Anthony was crusading, a new means of transportation was beginning to grow more popular. In particular, it provided much more mobility to women. *Anthony called it the single greatest development in the liberation of women—the bicycle!*

The prototype of the bicycle dates to the seventeenth century, possibly even earlier. These early types were propelled by running or walking, somewhat akin to a scooter. By the latter part of the nineteenth century, they had assumed much of their present character: rubber tires, wheels of equal size, and a pedal-chain drive. They emerged along with the automobile and only slightly before the airplane (the Wright brothers, of course, were bicycle builders and mechanics). The US Army experimented with their use, but abandoned the idea. The Japanese Army continued their use and found them highly useful in their rapid conquest of Southeast Asia during WWII. Bicycles were ideal for the quick transport of troops along jungle paths.

\*  \*  \*

Prior to two major changes in technology, political candidates and leaders depended on the print media and word-of-mouth communication to get their message across. While public speeches were very common, few could actually hear the speaker in large gatherings. The development of voice amplification (loud speakers) changed this, but the much more important change was the advent of broadcast radio. The landmark year was 1920 when broadcast stations began to emerge. The Netherlands, the United States, Canada, and Argentina were among the first to broadcast.

> Dr. G. says: KDKA in Pittsburgh is often cited as the first licensed broadcast station in the United States. At least one other station in Detroit, although unlicensed, was in operation about the same time.

Radio gave national leaders the ability to reach the public directly. Radio was an immense help in bringing Adolf Hitler to power—and in providing Churchill and Franklin D. Roosevelt the ability to rally people against him. The power of radio was made clear in 1938 when *Mercury Theatre on the Air* presented H. G. Wells's "War of the Worlds." The program set off somewhat of a public panic in the New York/New Jersey area where, according to the script, an invasion of Earth by undocumented aliens (presumably from Mars) in hovercraft was underway.

> Dr. G. says: FDR's fireside chats, a great source of inspiration and comfort to the American people, began with the request that listeners bring a map to their radio set. How many subsequent presidents have used maps in their public addresses?

Entertainers like Jack Benny, the Lone Ranger, Arthur Godfrey, and Ralph Edwards were immensely popular without anyone ever seeing them—until TV came along. I never did see *Ralph Edwards, but his radio program is forever enshrined in New Mexico, where a city, Truth or Consequences, is named after it.*

\* \* \*

One of my fellow graduate students presented an idea in a seminar to our department in about 1965. His claim was outrageous: he thought that within twenty years virtually everyone would use what was then called "pay TV." Why, I thought, would anyone willingly pay to have TV brought into his home when he could get it free with an antenna? I have often hoped that the graduate student in question profited greatly from his insight because not only did cable, and later satellite, home TV systems come into being, they arrived earlier than even his predictions. *The irony was that cable TV first achieved real commercial success in Pennsylvania, where mountains prevented TV broadcast signals from reaching many customers.* Indeed, I became an early customer in State College, Pennsylvania.

\* \* \*

The limited-access, long distance, high-speed highway that we now take for granted in the US Interstate Highway system was invented by the Germans in the form of their autobahns. The autobahn idea was developed in the Weimar Republic (Germany) in the 1920s but was brought to fruition by Adolf Hitler, who put more than 100,000 workers on the job building autobahns in the 1930s. In 1936, the greatest automobile speed ever achieved by an automobile on a public highway occurred on an autobahn—more than 270 mph.

*The autobahn concept was transferred to the United States in the late 1930s when Pennsylvania began construction on the Pennsylvania Turnpike. The first stretch was completed in 1940.*

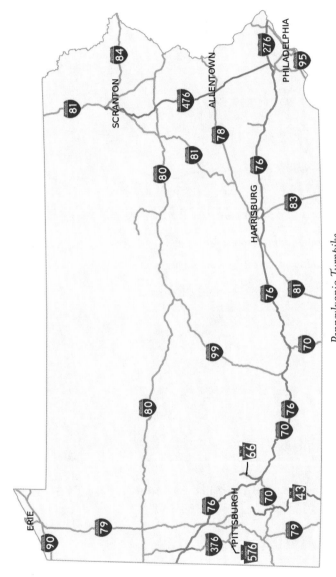

*Pennsylvania Turnpike*

# From Geography . . .

## . . . to Gastronomy

~

Food for Thought:

*"I don't like food that's too carefully arranged; it makes me think that the chef is spending too much time arranging and not enough time cooking."*

—Andy Rooney

~

**Recipe for:**

Meatloaf, Mashies, and Pea Salad (A Modern-Day TV Dinner)

# MEATLOAF, MASHIES, AND PEA SALAD

## (A Modern-Day TV Dinner)

*Serves 6–8*

When I was growing up, I think we all thought TV dinners were cool. I always got the battered fish or fish sticks (but I remember preferring the fillet). I never did like the warm applesauce. There were always other choices like Salisbury steak, fried chicken, or meatloaf, all with warm applesauce. Soon though, the novelty wore off—they were expensive to buy, and the food not so good.

This meatloaf is based on my mom's recipe—I just added more veggies and a few spices and don't cook it in a bread pan. Make sure you chop the vegetables into small pieces—this is why I use a food processor—otherwise, the meatloaf won't hold together as well. An added plus for those of you who have picky eaters is that they will be getting a mouthful of nutritious vegetables with every bite. I also glaze mine with barbecue sauce just before it is finished cooking, and since we're a sauce family, I serve extra at the table. The pea salad is one I made up after eating a similar one at Horatio's restaurant in Honolulu overlooking the harbor.

Just seems like this is one of those meals that everyone asks for again and again. The mashed potatoes, I have not included a recipe for. Just make your favorite kind—homemade or store bought—creamy and laced with just a hint of sour cream. Go ahead and throw in some roasted garlic or a sprinkling of fresh chives if you want to.

Here are some recipes to make a new memory of what a TV dinner should taste like.

# MOM'S UPDATED MEATLOAF

## INGREDIENTS

3 slices of bread (use whatever you have on hand—I like
   sourdough) torn up in small pieces

I cup of milk

2 eggs, lightly beaten

½ teaspoon Dijon mustard

½ teaspoon salt

I tablespoon Worcestershire sauce

3–4 dashes hot sauce (I use Frank's)

I lb. ground beef (I use 80%, but you can choose a leaner
   grind), thawed

I lb. ground sausage (I use Jimmy Dean "hot"), thawed

4 ribs of celery, buzzed in the food processor with the blade
   or diced

I small onion plus 2 cloves of garlic, buzzed in the food
   processor or diced

3 large carrots (or I cup), peeled and buzzed in the food
   processor or diced

I small fennel bulb, buzzed in the food processor or diced (if
   you don't have fennel, substitute ½ teaspoon fennel seeds

½ cup barbecue sauce plus additional for serving

## MY METHOD

Prepare a rimmed baking sheet and line with foil or line with parchment. This is mostly to make clean-up easier and totally optional.

In a large bowl, combine bread pieces with milk, eggs, mustard, salt, Worcestershire, and hot sauce. Stir to mix and let sit for 5 minutes.

Add in beef, pork, and vegetables, and using your hands, gently mix all together.

Divide into 2 equal portions and form them each into a loaf. Place them side by side, but not touching on the prepared baking sheet. You may also wrap and freeze them tightly in parchment, plastic, and foil, if you would like to make them ahead for another event.

Bake at 350°F for 45 minutes. Check the internal temperature with a thermometer. It should read 145°F for medium doneness (remember it will continue to cook for 10–15 minutes). Pull them out of the oven and give them a slathering of your favorite barbecue sauce and cook for 5 more minutes. Then shut off the oven and allow it to sit for another 10 minutes. Remove from oven and let stand for at least 10 minutes before slicing. Don't forget to serve with extra sauce!

# PEA SALAD

I have seen this salad with cheese or onions added, but this is the way I like it best.

## INGREDIENTS

2 lbs. peas, fresh or frozen (thawed and drained really well—I will squeeze out some of the moisture with paper towels). Do not use canned peas—they will ruin your pea salad experience.

1 lb. bacon, cooked until crumbly (go ahead and crumble them in a bowl)

2 cans sliced water chestnuts, drained and blotted

¾ cup mayonnaise

Salt and pepper to taste

## MY METHOD

Mix peas, bacon, and water chestnuts in a large bowl. Add in mayonnaise and stir until the peas are lightly coated. Sprinkle in the salt and pepper and give it another stir.

# SOUTHERN LATITUDES

*Question 135: Who was the first European to discover New Zealand?*

*Question 136: What word is used to describe the kangaroo, opossum, bandicoot, and wallaby?*

*Question 137: What country occupies the most degrees of southern latitude?*

*Question 138: Is Sri Lanka north or south of the equator?*

*Question 139: What three South American countries are crossed by the equator?*

*Question 140: In what country can you find Robben Island?*

*Question 141: How do you make Not-so-Trite Shrimp on the Barbie?*

During the age of exploration, a number of prominent thinkers were convinced that there had to be a large land mass in the Southern Hemisphere to maintain the earth's balance. There was so much land north of the equator, they hypothesized that a great continent, which they called "Terra Australias," must exist in the south. Eventually, I presume, they were satisfied with the discovery of Australia and Antarctica. Still, even with these two continents, the Southern Hemisphere has a dearth of land, particularly in the range of 40 to 60 degrees south latitude. Consequently, there is little land to interrupt wind or current here, and ships often encounter treacherous seas in these latitudes.

Among the first to explore in the southern latitudes of the Pacific was Dutch explorer Abel Tasman. The Dutch were interested in spices, more, presumably, than they already had in the Spice Islands of the Dutch East Indies. *Tasman sailed south of Australia, in mountainous seas, and discovered the island named after him—Tasmania (although Tasman named it Van Diemen's Land). He went on to discover New Zealand,* although because longitude could not be properly measured at sea, Tasman thought he was in Argentina! (As poor navigation as this is, it is better than Columbus's confusion of the Caribbean Islands with Asia.)

\*    \*    \*

It was Captain James Cook in the ship *Endeavour,* and the noted botanist on board, Joseph Banks, who opened up Australia to settlement. They discovered the eastern coast of Australia, and, after only this brief encounter, Britain decided it was the perfect place to transport criminals who were clogging up their prisons. Actually, the British had sent the bulk of their prisoners to the North American colonies, but the success of the American Revolution had put a stop to that. The plants and animals found on early explorations to Australia were unique to the island continent and, in some cases, were greatly doubted back in England. A common expression in Britain was "as rare as a black swan" since a black swan was considered impossible—but there really were black swans in Australia. The first platypus sent back to Britain as a zoological specimen was initially thought to be a practical joke! *Many of the animals discovered there such as the kangaroo, bandicoot, wallaby, and opossum were marsupial mammals,* meaning that the young were born live in an embryonic state and nurtured in the mother's external pouch.

\*    \*    \*

Depending on how the measurement is done, California, were it an independent country, would have one of the world's largest economies (probably 12th ranking). The Southern Hemisphere counterpart to California is Chile—but almost everything California has Chile has to a greater extent. Chile's Atacama Desert is drier than Death Valley, the Andes are higher than the Sierras, and Chile's coastline is much longer than California's. In fact, *Chile has the longest north-south dimension of any country in the Southern Hemisphere.* Chile, however, although a reasonably prosperous country by world standards (and growing more so) lacks California's connectivity, both internationally and domestically. While Chile has tremendous agricultural and tourism potential, competitors are invariably closer to major international markets.

To reach the Southern Hemisphere from the north, it is of course necessary to cross the equator; once we do, things change to a surprising degree. Summer changes magically to winter, and fall to spring. Sundials don't work as they are supposed to, and the English speaking natives (at least those in Australia) speak of a "uni" instead of a university and an "esky" as a portable place to keep things cold. "Barbie" is probably too trite to mention, but there is apparently something about southern latitudes that cause words to be shortened. Religious symbolism is topsy-turvy as well since Easter, symbolized by the resurrection of nature in the spring, occurs in the fall. Christmas, associated with the Roman Saturnalia, the celebration of the sun's rising after the solstice on about December 21, loses its symbolism in the Southern Hemisphere, where the days begin to shorten after the solstice. As strange as all this may be, it becomes even more mystifying when we realize that the exact location of the equator is rather vague in our minds.

Having led oodles of tourists around locations in Hawaii, I can testify that many are surprised to learn that Hawaii is in the North Pacific Ocean, not the South Pacific—and a few are disappointed. We learn from all kinds of sources (especially movies) that India is a hot tropical land with elephants, tigers, and cobras. Sri Lanka (formerly Ceylon), which hangs south of India sort of like a pendant, is even more tropical. Most of my university students, when asked to draw the equator over a map of the Indian subcontinent, will draw it directly over central India, or even a bit to the north. *Both India and Sri Lanka, however, are northern hemisphere countries; the equator is south of both of them in the Indian Ocean.*

\*   \*   \*

The equator's location in South America is oh so easy to find because we named a country after it! The equator passes through Ecuador. But what other countries does it pass through? The answer to almost any geographic question about South America seems to be Brazil—it is so big! In this case, it is the right answer; the equator does indeed pass through Brazil. It is the third country, however, that only about one student in a hundred can name (at least without some homework). It is Colombia.

> Dr. G. says: I was once asked to deliver a talk about Columbus's exploration of Colombia. It would have been a very short talk because, although the country is named for Columbus, he was never there.

\*   \*   \*

> Dr. G. says: In South Africa, politicians tend to serve prison time before election, while in the United States, prison time seems to follow election. Perhaps this is another strange effect of the equator (but I doubt it).

*Robben Island is a tiny island near Cape Town, South Africa.* Its existence would have escaped the notice of even the most devout trivia player were it not for the fact that Nobel Laureate and former South African president Nelson Mandela was imprisoned for eighteen years on the island. Three presidents served time there before being elected.

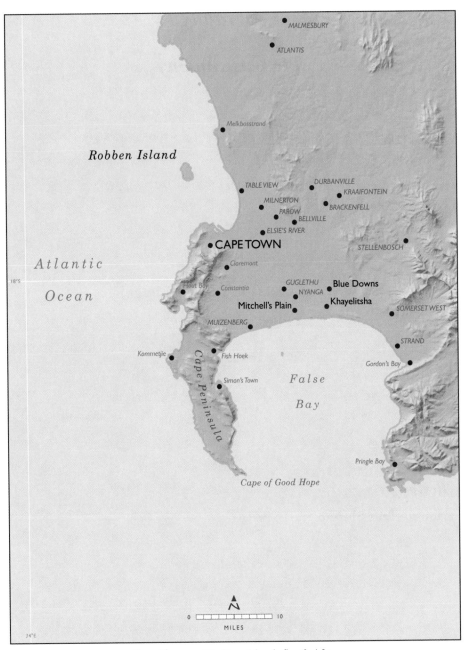

Cape Town and Robben Island, South Africa

# From Geography . . .

## . . . to Gastronomy

~

Food for Thought:

*"Tis an ill cook that cannot lick his own fingers."*

—William Shakespeare

~

## Recipe for:

Not-so-Trite Shrimp on the Barbie

# NOT-SO-TRITE SHRIMP ON THE BARBIE

*Serves 8 as a main course or 10–12 as an appetizer*

Too hard to pass this one up! This is a great make-ahead dish to use for a large gathering, a picnic or event. Serve with pasta tossed with pesto, a rice pilaf, or a crusty baguette.

## INGREDIENTS

**3 lbs. 36 size shrimp, peeled, deveined, leaving tails intact**
**¼ cup EVOO**
**½ cup dry white wine, a good drinking Chardonnay**
**¼ cup fresh lemon juice**
**2 teaspoons salt**
**8–10 dashes of hot sauce**
**3–4 garlic cloves, minced**
**Serve with fresh lemon wedges**

## MY METHOD

Combine all ingredients into a large bowl. Cover to coat evenly. Allow to marinate for at least an hour and up to 2, but no more—otherwise you will have ceviche (shrimp cooked in acidity).

Thread on skewers and grill or bake on baking sheets for 2 minutes on each side, turning. They really do cook quickly! Do not overcook or you will have rubbery shrimp. Enjoy!

# SETTLEMENT OF THE PACIFIC: THE FINAL FRONTIER

*(I want to boldly go) "farther than any man has been before me."*

—James Cook

*Question 142: Of the settled continents, which was the last to receive human habitation?*

*Question 143: What plant was the* **Bounty** *transporting at the time of the famous mutiny?*

*Question 144: What Pacific island has the world's greatest density of languages—the most different languages per square mile?*

*Question 145: Genes for blonde hair are native to Scandinavia and what region of the Pacific?*

*Question 146: More than 90 percent of Polynesia's land area is found in what country?*

*Question 147: How do you make Pineapple-Papaya Salsa?*

By the end of the last Ice Age (roughly 11,000 years ago), all the inhabitable continents had been settled. *South America was last,* probably receiving its first humans just as the ice was beginning to retreat. Many assume that Australia, because of its isolation, was only recently settled, but people have lived in Australia for around

Dr. G. says: A notable exception to this was Iceland, which was first settled in about 870 AD.

50,000 years. Only the Pacific, roughly one-third of the earth's surface, lacked people.

Most of the Pacific Islands lacked vegetation and animals that could provide enough food for a human population. The people that were to settle this final frontier therefore had to have developed agriculture—and they had to take their domestic plants and animals with them. Without a doubt, many early settlement efforts failed, but if crops could be planted and animals released, subsequent settlement efforts had a much better chance of survival.

Dr. G. says: This practice is the origin, I believe, of the Polynesian word "taboo." Plants and animals taken on a voyage to a new island could not be eaten along the way, no matter how great the temptation. Priests would place a taboo on the cargo; breaking a taboo would mean death.

The breadfruit offers a particularly appropriate example. This plant provided one of the principal foods for Pacific island people. It is believed to have originated in New Guinea and was carried eastward into the Pacific by ancestors of the Polynesians. In the Pacific, the plant is incredibly prolific and a mature plant can produce hundreds of grapefruit-sized breadfruit in a season. It takes years, however, for a plant to reach the fruiting stage. Planting breadfruit, then, offered hope for the future rather than an immediate food supply.

Were there plants on some islands, prior to human occupation, that could provide a food source? Perhaps, but the breadfruit provides yet another example. The British, and to a lesser extent, the French, encountered the breadfruit in early voyages of exploration and hit on the idea of planting breadfruit in the Caribbean as a food source for slaves working on sugar plantations. Most Caribbean slaves, however, would not eat breadfruit. Food choices are based on deeply held cultural norms, and there is abundant evidence to show that people will starve to death rather than eat plants or animals that they do not consider "food." In any case, the main food items in the Polynesian diet were brought with them. *In fact, it was the mission of the Bounty, commanded by Captain Bligh, to carry breadfruit seedlings to the Caribbean, an unsuccessful mission as it turned out.*

Dr. G. says: A strange exception to this is Puerto Rico, where breadfruit was accepted and became part of the local cuisine.

The term "Polynesia," meaning "many islands," first coined in the 1750s, was once applied to all the Pacific Islands. Later, a finer distinction was drawn: "Melanesia" (black islands) and Micronesia (little islands) were thrown into the mix. These labels were developed by Europeans, looking at the island Pacific through European eyes. While these terms are not unreasonable, since they reflect both locational and cultural factors, the reality is that the native population of the Pacific all originated in Taiwan, all coped with a fairly similar environment, and, in general, their similarities may be greater than their differences.

Melanesia was the first region settled and, not surprisingly, has the oldest languages. What is surprising, however, is the number of languages. New Caledonia, for example, with an area of only 7,000 sq. miles, has thirty-five languages. *Vanuatu, with an area of only about 4,000 square miles, has 119 native languages, the highest language density of any place on earth.*

Culture, our learned behavior transmitted from one generation to the next, strongly unites those who share it in common and separates us from those who do not share it. Language is, on the one hand, the most unifying, and on the other, the most divisive aspect of culture. We feel a strong bond with people who speak our language—especially if they share our dialect, accent, and nonverbal cues. The language mosaic of Vanuatu and, indeed, the rest of Melanesia can only be accounted for by the isolation of one settlement from another—an isolation that must have endured for a long time. With such linguistic diversity in such a relatively small area, conflict was common.

> Dr. G. says: A British anthropologist once told me that "what football (soccer) is to Britain, warfare was to Melanesia."

Some means of communication between different language groups must have developed in the past, but the common languages, pidgins that exist in Melanesia today, show the strong influence of European trade and colonization. Vanuatu's pidgin, Bislama, is one of the world's most unusual languages. It developed as a result of the sea slug trade between Vanuatu and China; Bislama derives from the French for sea slug, *beche le mer*.

Melanesia provided something of a dilemma for European colonizers. Most of Melanesia is outside the area of deep basaltic rock that characterizes much of the Pacific Basin. It therefore has valuable minerals—gold, nickel, and copper in particular. On the other hand, the natives were reputed to be savage cannibals. Cannibalism is a highly controversial subject today. Many (probably most) anthropologists argue that it is the invention of European minds. There is, however, strong evidence of its existence and wide-spread practice.

*Melanesia also has one other unusual feature. Genes for blonde hair originated only in Norway—and Melanesia.*

*Blonde hair in Melanesia*

\*    \*    \*

The Polynesian Triangle encompasses millions of square miles in the Pacific, but actually has a small land area. *More than 90 percent of Polynesia's land is found in New Zealand.* Polynesia extends from Hawaii in the north, to New Zealand in the southwest, to Rapa Nui (Easter Island) in the southeast. Polynesian settlement in the extreme points of this triangle represent an incredible accomplishment—voyages of exploration and settlement over thousands of miles of open ocean.

Polynesian settlement has been recent, conquering earth's last settlement frontier. New Zealand is almost certainly the last settled place; Polynesians arrived in New Zealand in about 1250 AD. Despite New Zealand's substantial land area, the native Polynesians—Maori—lacked a stable food supply and their population was therefore restricted. Traditional Polynesian foods—coconut, taro, breadfruit, banana— would not grow in New Zealand's nontropical climate.

Dr. G. says: The Maori could grow a sweet potato, ku-mara, even on the South Island. The sweet potato is native to Central America and exactly how it got to New Zealand has stimulated much speculation.

The large birds unique to New Zealand, moa, were driven to ex-tinction by hunting. At about the time the moa died out, Europeans arrived with potatoes, which did provide greater food security.

Hawaii, while much smaller in land area than New Zealand, had a considerably larger population before Europeans arrived. The official estimate is about 350,000, but some scholars have argued for a population of at least twice that number—or more. Initially, Captain Cook and other early arrivers limited their exploration to the leeward sides of the islands—where it was safest to sail. We now know, however, that the windward sides of the islands contained the most people. Why were so many people in Hawaii? It had abundant freshwater sources, lots of reasonably level land for cultivation, and shoreline locations where fish ponds could be built.

Despite the fact that they are scattered over an immense area, Polynesian languages are quite similar, as the chart below shows. Such differences that exist can be accounted for by three main fac-tors: 1) no Polynesian culture had a written language. Alphabets and writing systems were developed by Europeans or Americans, often missionaries, who assigned letters to the sounds they heard in the native languages. What sounded like an *r* to one sounded like an *l* to another, or was that a *w* or a *v* sound?; 2) words dropped out of the language and new ones, based on contact with outsid-ers, developed. Sixty percent of Hawaiian words had disappeared by 1850, while new words, like "luau" (for a feast), date only to the late nineteenth century; 3) some "drift" in language was bound to occur as Polynesian people lost contact with one another due to their spread over the Pacific.

## Language Similarities in the Pacific for Numbers 1–10

|    | Maori | Hawaiian | Tongan | Samoan | Fijian | Tahitian |
|----|-------|----------|--------|--------|--------|----------|
| 1  | tahi  | kahi     | taha   | tasi   | dua    | ho'e     |
| 2  | rua   | lua      | ua     | lua    | rua    | piti     |
| 3  | toru  | kolu     | tolu   | tolu   | tolu   | toru     |
| 4  | wha   | ha       | fa     | fa     | va     | maha     |
| 5  | rima  | lima     | nima   | lima   | lima   | pae      |
| 6  | ono   | ono      | ono    | ono    | ono    | ono      |
| 7  | whitu | hiku     | fitu   | fitu   | vitu   | hitu     |
| 8  | waru  | walu     | valu   | valu   | valu   | va'u     |
| 9  | iwa   | iwa      | hiva   | iva    | ciwa   | iva      |
| 10 | tekau | -'umi    | -fulu  | sefulu | tini   | 'ahuru   |

*Table created by Barbara Fuller.*

Captain James Cook, a geographer and ship captain, was the most noted of the Pacific explorers. He undertook three incredible voyages (see map below). His first voyage took him first to Tahiti, where he built a shore observatory to observe the transit of Venus in 1769.

> Dr. G. says: I first heard of the transit of Venus as a sophomore in high school when a fellow student, with an interest in physics and astronomy, mentioned it during a discussion of a related phenomenon, parallax. The teacher assumed it was something pornographic and took appropriate action.

The transit of Venus is not well understood by most. It is the period of time during which Venus is visible from the earth as it passes across the face of the sun. In the eighteenth century, the ratio of planetary orbits was well understood, but no one knew the "solar constant," the distance from earth to the sun. Once that

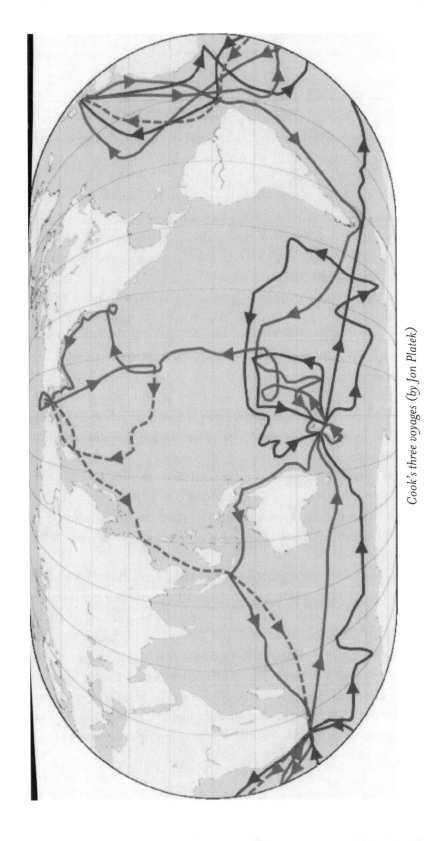

*Cook's three voyages (by Jon Platek)*

could be calculated, then we would know how far each planet was from the sun and, hence, the size of the solar system. If the transit of Venus were to be observed and timed from many points of earth, the solar constant could be determined. In fact, the experiment didn't work. In Cook's case (and probably in others as well), it was hard to tell exactly when Venus entered the face of the sun and when it exited. Looking back on the history of the measurement attempt, it is likely that any reasonably accurate calculations would have been dismissed. At the time, scientists could not conceive that the sun was 93 million miles away!

Cook went on to circumnavigate and map New Zealand (thereby proving it was insular) and was the first European to land on the east coast of Australia. The bay in which Cook anchored eventually was named Botany Bay because of the unique flora discovered and categorized by the botanist aboard, Joseph Banks. It was Banks, rather than Cook, who gained great credit and fame for the voyage commanded by Cook. Banks was considered the British expert on Australia and was primarily responsible for the idea of sending prisoners there.

On Cook's third voyage, he discovered the final corner of the Polynesian Triangle, Hawaii. He landed first on the island of Kauai, then went on to Alaska, and finally returned to Hawaii, this time to Kealakekua Bay on Hawaii Island. Cook was killed on the beach there in a dispute with Hawaiians.

European and Americans who were early arrivals in Hawaii heard stories that the Hawaiians had traveled from the Society Islands, but the stories were not believable. Not only did it seem impossible to travel such a distance in canoes, but how could finding locations in the Pacific be done without the maps and navigational equipment that the foreigners had? The Polynesian voyages of discovery and settlement really do seem miraculous, but the real mystery seems to be: why did they stop making such voyages? By the time of Cook's first contact, Hawaii had no long-range voyaging canoes and (apparently) no navigators.

# From Geography...

## ...to Gastronomy

~

Food for Thought:

*"Borders? I have never seen one. But I have heard they exist in the minds of some people."*

—Thor Heyerdahl

~

## Recipe for:

Pineapple-Papaya Salsa

# PINEAPPLE-PAPAYA SALSA

*Makes about 4 cups*

This tropical and fruity salsa is perfect with grilled or baked fish, teriyaki style pork or chicken, or just with salty tortilla chips.

## INGREDIENTS

3 cups diced pineapple

2 ripe papaya, peeled, seeded, and diced

1 cup minced red onion

2 serrano chili peppers, seeded and minced (make sure to use gloves—be very careful to not touch the seeds—they are very hot!)

½ cup fresh lime juice

1 large bunch freshly chopped cilantro leaves

1 teaspoon hot chili oil

## MY METHOD

Combine all ingredients in a medium bowl and allow to sit for at least 20 minutes to allow flavors to mingle. Can be made up to 2 hours in advance. This is best eaten fresh on the day it is made.

# THE DAIRY BELT

*Question 148: Why is vitamin D added to milk?*

*Question 149: How do farmers engaged in market agriculture decide what to grow?*

*Question 150: What kind of cow has "udderly" taken over milk production in the United States?*

*Question 151: What kind of cow was the symbol for Borden?*

*Question 152: Where is the dairy belt?*

*Question 153: How do you make Vanilla Ricotta Cheese?*

Milk was the "Elixir of Life" when I was a boy. The area where I at-tended school in northern New York state, *had a reputation for rickets (vitamin D deficiency), and since milk was fortified with vitamin D by the dairies,* we all had to drink a half pint whether we wanted it, paid for it, or detested it. As nearly as I could tell, everyone drank their milk with relish—in fact, I don't think I met anyone growing up who did not drink milk. Other dairy products were more problematic.

My parents would not eat butter. It wasn't that they didn't like it, or thought it bad for them, but rather that they *did* like butter—the butter they had grown up churning at home. They claimed dairy-produced butter was all but inedible. So, like a great many other families, we bought plastic bags filled with white goo. My job was to break open a small pack of yellow dye on the side of the bag and knead and knead until the mass turned yellow. The resulting mass resembled butter and (in my neighborhood) was called "oleo." Others called it margarine, and people from the South I met in later life called it "margaREEN." Later, of course, margarine took the stick or tub form we know today.

Cheese was another matter entirely. No one I knew in my early years liked cheese of any kind—with the possible exception of cream cheese. Cream cheese was an American invention, as was Limburger, which German families ate. Macaroni and cheese, now a mainstay of kids' diets, was universally detested by any child I grew up with. Then, one day, when I was about ten years old, my family and I were driving to attend a funeral being conducted in a highly rural area on the western edges of the Tug Hill Plateau in New York. We got dreadfully lost. My father stopped to ask directions at what proved to be a cheese factory. He came back to the car with directions, extra-sharp cheddar cheese, and cheese curd. I was assured that cheese curd really wasn't cheese and therefore tried some. It was salty rubber—but absolutely delicious. My mother later made me a cheeseburger—my first—with the cheddar. The cheese made my mouth tingle, but it was also delicious and nothing like the American cheese that was more common.

Now for a taste of geographic theory! In the early nineteenth century a German economic geographer, von Thünen, asked a basic question: why virtually all the farmers in a given area grow the same crop, while farmers in another area produce a different crop. Then, as now, farmers were known to be cantankerous and independent—why would neighboring farmers agree on what crop to grow (or product to make)? When we confront the same question, answers like soil fertility, climate, water availability, and similar physical or natural factors spring to mind. The region that von Thünen was looking at, however, was a rather small area in south Germany where climate, soil fertility, and the cultural preferences for food were all the same.

Von Thünen made a number of assumptions, the most reasonable of which was (in my opinion) that the farmers would produce that which would give them the most profit per acre. In the imaginary, but perfect, conditions von Thünen hypothesized (which he called the Isolated State), the farmers were not subsistence farmers (that is, raising things for their own use), but market farmers. He used the idea of economic rent, which means that farm land nearest a market city needs to produce a lot of output per acre (essentially competing with the high price of land near the urban area). The price to ship each unit of farm production to the market might be high, but there wasn't much distance to cover. Considering only dairy products, this location near the market is perfect for the production of whole milk. In the case of more distant farms, transport costs begin to play a bigger role. The farmer needs a product with a higher value per unit of weight to overcome the influence of distance. As a parallel example, consider that shipping me a roll of paper towels for a Christmas present makes little sense; the postage would cost more than the towels. On the other hand, sending me a bag of diamonds (from anywhere) is economically feasible. Butter is more valuable per unit of weight than milk, so we would expect more distant farmers to produce butter, and those even more distant farms to turn their milk into cheese.

> Dr. G. says: As I've told my students, there's no substitute for hands-on experience with geographic theory. If you'd like to try this yourself, I will be glad to furnish an address where you can ship the paper towels and the diamonds.

In von Thünen's Isolated State, as one moves farther and farther from the market, it will eventually not be profitable to raise dairy cows at all. Some other crop will be chosen, or crops will be grown only for subsistence.

> Dr. G. says: Both the Jersey and the Guernsey come, of course, from the English Channel Islands of the same names. The other large Channel Island, however, is Sark. I have never heard of a Sark cow.

> Dr. G. says: An Australian cattle dealer I met read about my comparison of a Jersey cow with a golden retriever and entirely agreed with me. On the other hand, he informed me, the Jersey bull is like a pit bull. His stories of the ferocity of Jersey bulls made me wonder why Spanish matadors and Texas cowboys never mix it up with Jersey bulls.

I have often wondered whether breeds of dairy cattle are distributed much as fluid milk, butter, and cheese are distributed in the Isolated State. Jerseys and Guernseys produce milk with a high butter fat content. Readers of my earlier book will recall that I am particularly fond of Jerseys, while I lament the fate of the Guernsey; this cow has been made obsolete! Elsie and Elmer, *Guernseys, were the symbols of Borden.* Their milk was noted for being slightly yellow in color, and highly prized at one time. Butter fat, however, became the bane of the American housewife. *In place of these gentle cattle came the larger and more proficient Holstein Friesian.* The amount of milk that can be produced by a prized Holstein is incredible—and the lower butter fat content of Holsteins, the happier the contemporary consumers. Were there a magazine called *Playbull*, the Holstein Frisian would be the centerfold. I would expect Jerseys and Guernseys might be in the nether regions of the dairy belt, far from the market and perhaps in areas where specialty cheeses are produced.

*The traditional dairy belt in the United States extends from New England, across upstate New York, through Michigan and Wisconsin to include parts of Minnesota.* The belt, however, is breaking down. Dairy farms are being sold for housing—or being abandoned—in ever increasing numbers. Meanwhile, mini-dairy belts are developing around large cities in the South and West.

Why is there a dairy belt at all in North America—and a similar belt across northern Europe? Nomadic herders across Europe, Asia, and Africa have used the milk from their herds for thousands of years, but certain European tribes eventually ceased their nomad-ism, became sedentary, but kept their animals and their milk. About the time that dairy herds developed, some people began to develop what is called lactase persistence, that is, they could continue to easily digest milk even when they became adults. About 50 percent of the world's population holds this genetic trait.

Regions with high
concentrations
of dairy cows

Primary

Secondary

*D a i r y   B e l t*

N

MILES

0                    400

*The dairy belt*

# From Geography . . .

# . . . to Gastronomy

∼

### Food for Thought:

*"You can unite the French only through fear. You cannot simply bring together a country that has over 265 kinds of cheese."*

—Charles de Gaulle

∼

### Recipe for:

Vanilla Ricotta Cheese

# VANILLA RICOTTA CHEESE

*Makes just under 2 cups of cheese*

If you have never made cheese, this is the easiest recipe to get you to try your hand at making some. Make this cheese for a special appetizer or dessert. Use it to stuff cannoli (try the recipe in chapter II). Use it to dollop on a slice of toasted baguette, a slice of strawberry, a chiffonade of mint, and a drizzle of balsamic reduction.

## INGREDIENTS

4 cups whole milk

2 cups heavy cream

½ vanilla bean, scraped (use the scraped seeds and reserve the pod for another use)

I teaspoon kosher salt

3 tablespoons apple cider vinegar

## MY METHOD

Set a large colander lined with cheesecloth over a deep bowl or another pot.

Pour the milk and cream into a heavy-bottomed pot. Stir in the vanilla seeds and salt. Bring to a full boil over medium heat, stirring occasionally. Remove from heat. Stir in the vinegar. Let it set and wait one minute until it curdles. Gently and slowly stir a few times.

Pour the mixture into the colander and give it time to drain into the bowl, about 25 minutes. The ricotta can be refrigerated for up to 5 days in an airtight container.

*Vanilla ricotta*
*(photo by T. M. Reddekopp)*

# WHAT'S IN A NAME?

.........................................................

*Question 154: Where is the largest Native American reservation in the United States and to what nation does it belong?*

*Question 155: What Native American tribe has a reservation completely surrounded by the reservation in question #154?*

*Question 156: In what US state is Mesa Verde National Park?*

*Question 157: In what kind of business establishment can we find the Code Talkers Museum?*

*Question 158: What Native American language spoken in the southwestern United States is unrelated to any other known language?*

*Question 159: How do you make Three Sisters' Pudding?*

.........................................................

> Dr. G. says: In the course of my research career, I have had editors blue-pencil "manhole covers" and "mangrove swamps" on the grounds that they are "reactionary sexist expressions."

It's strange that the politically correct movement has not taken on the issue of creature's names. "Killer whale," for example, seems terribly unfair since we have not convicted a single one of homicide. But how would you like to go through life known as a "False Killer Whale" or a "Lesser Kudu"? Surely this must lead to self-esteem issues. When it comes to people, however, geographers have to tread carefully because groups of people are constantly disappearing from our maps. In the Far North, for example, Eskimos and Lapps have become Inuit and Sami, while it still seems all right to refer to "Eskimo languages" and "Lapland." "Pakistani" is said to be highly offensive, but "Pakistan" is still the name of the country. In the United States, there seems to be constant tension between "Indian" and "Native American," and even more so when the Washington, DC, football team (which plays in Maryland) is considered. The team name "Redskins" is attacked, particularly when they have a losing season, but a high school on the Navajo reservation calls its sports teams "Redskins."

> Dr. G. says: Just as this was written, California outlawed the use of "Redskins" as a nickname for public school athletic teams. Four schools were affected.

The Navajo people and their reservation deserve a lot more attention in geography texts than they get (which is just about zero). *The Navajo Nation is the largest of all US Indian groups, and their reservation, which occupies the northeast corner of Arizona and adjacent land in New Mexico and Utah, is the largest reservation in the United States.* What is really remarkable about the Navajo, however, is that they won a huge victory over the US government—not on the battlefield, but under the treaty of 1868, which restored most of their land that had been taken from them. Like many other tribes, the Navajo had been forcibly removed from their land, and their homes and herds destroyed.

For years, I had taught about the Anasazi as ancestors of the Navajo and other southwestern US tribes. "Anasazi" is, in fact, a Diné (Navajo) word that is often translated as "ancient ones." The Anasazi built settlements, most notably cliff dwellings, across the Southwest, but then abandoned them and moved out around 1300 AD. However, on a recent trip to the Anasazi region, I discovered they had moved out a second time. The word Anasazi has apparently become politically incorrect and has been replaced by "Ancestral Puebloans," a phrase which not only tied my tongue but boggled my mind. While the contemporary Pueblo people are descended from the Anasazi, so are other Southwest groups.

Another group likely related to the Anasazi is the Hopi. *Their reservation is also in northeastern Arizona and is completely surrounded by the Navajo reservation.* This geographic anomaly is similar to San Marino (completely surrounded by Italy) and Lesotho (surrounded by South Africa). In the American Southwest where water and grazing land have been keys to survival, the juxtaposition of the two reservations was bound to generate disputes—and they have ever since the reservations were established.

Many of the Anasazi cliff dwellings are in Mesa Verde National Park, a truly spectacular place to visit. A great many of the Anasazi dwellings, however, are found outside the park, some as far south as the vicinity of Flagstaff, Arizona. *The park itself, however, is in Colorado.*

*Code Talkers Museum, Navajo Reservation, Arizona (photo by bbf)*

In recent years, a contribution of the Navajo people has become widely known and honored. During WWII, Navajos were used as radiomen by the US Marine Corps in the Pacific, perhaps most notably during the battle for Iwo Jima. Not all Navajo speak the same dialect, so it was necessary for the Navajo radiomen to develop a code for battlefield conditions—one that used words that all the radiomen recognized. The secrecy that surrounded this operation prevented public acknowledgment of this Navajo contribution for many years. Worse, perhaps, was the fact that Navajo code talkers did not receive the veteran benefits accorded other US servicemen. *The Code Talkers Museum is located in Kayenta, Arizona, on the Navajo reservation, and is in a Burger King restaurant.*

Geographers who specialize in the origin and spread of languages often point to the Basque region of Spain and France as a real anomaly. The Basque language is unrelated to any other European language or, for that matter, any other language anywhere. A similar situation exists in the American Southwest where the Zuni language is spoken. *Zuni is unrelated to any language of nearby groups, and, so far, linguists have been unable to link it to any other language anywhere.*

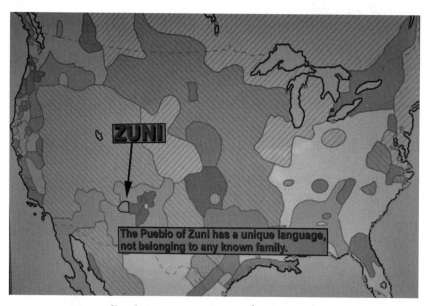

*Zuni language area, Arizona (photo by bbf)*

# From Geography . . .

*Canyon De Chelly, Arizona (photo by bbf)*

# . . . to Gastronomy

*Three sisters' pudding (photo by bbf)*

~

Food for Thought:

*"All plants are our brothers and sisters.*
*They talk to us, and if we listen, we can hear them."*

—Arapaho saying

~

**Recipe for:**

Three Sisters' Pudding

# THREE SISTERS' PUDDING

*Serves 6–8*

Corn, squash, and beans are considered the trinity of Native Americans—each supports the others to grow and to provide nutrients to one another and to return back to the soil. This is soul warming and a hearty, nourishing dish.

## INGREDIENTS

2 large zucchinis, diced fine or shredded through a food processor

4 cups corn, cut from the cob, and milk squeezed from the cobs as well

1 medium yellow bell pepper, diced fine or chopped in the food processor, divided

16 oz. bag frozen baby lima beans, thawed

Whole milk or cream, ¼ cup (optional)

¼ cup shelled sunflower seeds, plus additional for a garnish

Salt and pepper

## MY METHOD

Spread the zucchini into a colander, sprinkle with a teaspoon of salt, and allow to sit for 10 minutes. Squeeze out some of the moisture, but not until dry.

Pour the corn and corn-milk, zucchini, half of the bell pepper, lima beans, and sunflower seeds into a blender, or you can use an immersion blender or potato masher. Blend until creamy or until desired consistency, adding milk or cream if desired.

Melt butter over medium heat in a medium, heavy-bottomed saucepan. Add in mixture and the remaining half of bell pepper. Simmer until heated through or until it achieves desired thickness.

Serve with extra butter, Frank's hot sauce, and additional sunflower seeds.

An heirloom tomato salad drizzled with some good oil, vinegar of choice, a chiffonade of basil, and salt and pepper would make a fresh accompaniment.

# MY EARLY GEOGRAPHIC
# EDUCATION AND
# FIRST MIGRATION

*Question 160: Are both the North and South Poles at sea level?*

*Question 161: Thomas Dewey was twice Republican candidate for president, governor of New York, and an advisor to President Eisenhower. What was his hometown?*

*Question 162: Where was Mark Twain's summer home, Quarry Farm?*

*Question 163: Where is the Little League World Series played?*

*Question 164: The Piper Cub was the Ford Model T of aircraft, but it was not black but yellow. What city was its shade of yellow named after?*

*Question 165: How do you make Stovetop "Baked" Beans?*

I hope your early geographic education was better than mine. While I suppose there was a bit of geography taught in my early school years (I remember world maps on the wall), my first contact with something actually called "geography" was in ninth grade. The class should have been called "World Misinformation." Prior to this class, I believed that teachers were near god-like in their knowledge, so, at least at first, I believed every word the teacher said. To begin at the beginning, Adam and Eve were white, I learned, an assertion I have never heard elsewhere. Further, the earth was heated at the equator, exactly like a potbelly stove. The heat rose, that is, into the Northern Hemisphere, which certainly was "up" on the map she drew. How the Southern Hemisphere was heated was not mentioned. My personal geographic crisis came when we were taught that the sky was blue because so much of the earth was blue seawater—it reflected into the sky. I knew this wasn't correct, so I copied articles from six reference sources and, thus armed, privately explained to the teacher why the sky was really blue. The next exam asked why the sky was blue and the "seawater" nonsense was the only acceptable answer.

Another gem of ninth grade geography, and one I believed for years, was that the North and South Poles were open stretches of ocean, not frozen because seawater, containing salt, does not freeze. The "ice" we see in polar locations is actually freshwater—icebergs, for example, are freshwater and therefore float on the more dense and unfrozen seawater. This line of reasoning was accepted by geographers in roughly 1850 and continued in vogue for maybe thirty years afterward. Icebergs, of course, are freshwater, but seawater certainly freezes. This may come as a shock: *the South Pole is actually more than 9,000 feet above sea level. The highest point in Antarctica—about 750 miles from the pole—is over 16,000 feet in elevation. The North Pole is at sea level (please don't quibble about the ice on top).*

This early geographic experience eventually led to two principles of teaching that I shared with my university students each semester: 1) Never take my word for anything. Check for yourself anything I allege. If I ever offer an opinion, ignore it; and 2) you are responsible for your own education. No matter how bad the teacher, professor, or textbook, you have to figure out a way to learn. After you have learned, work to get the textbook burned and the professor fired.

\* \* \*

As a child, I learned about an Eden, a place I never saw but which my parents had often visited and, every now and then, would reminisce about. My paternal grandmother had seven sisters. I met several of my great aunts—all impressive women—but one I never met lived in this idyllic place: Pawling, New York, on the east side of the Hudson River, an exurb of New York City. When I became old enough to investigate Pawling, I was startled at the famous people who lived there: Lowell Thomas and Edward R. Murrow alone amazed me. Both were voices that narrated WWII to the American public via radio and newsreels.

*Perhaps the most famous resident of Pawling, however, was Thomas E. Dewey.* Dewey was the Republican candidate for president in 1944, running against the incumbent president, Franklin Delano Roosevelt. FDR might have been beaten for his second term in 1936 (he actually won by a landslide) or for his unprecedented third term in 1940. While WWII still raged, it seemed impossible, however, for the Republicans to unseat FDR in his quest for a fourth term in 1944. In fact, while Roosevelt did win, Dewey came closer to winning than any previous candidate. In 1948, however, Dewey seemed a shoo-in. Everyone expected him to easily defeat Harry Truman. On election night, Pawling was prepared to celebrate when their native son was elected president of the United States. Fire sirens were to scream and fireworks paint the sky. The next day, however, Pawling was very quiet as it turned out Truman had won! Perhaps there was no joy in Mudville, but there was even less in Pawling when Dewey struck out.

\*    \*    \*

Americans migrate, on average, about once every five years. By "migrate" I mean they change residence across a county line and remain in the new residence for at least a year.

> Dr. G. says: That's the US Census definition of migration.

About the last thing I ever expected to do was move after my wife and I had obtained good post-college jobs in the central New York

*Albert Fuller (left), father and grandfather of the authors, meets with New York governor Thomas E. Dewey (center, in dark suit) at the signing of contracts for the construction of the New York State Thruway.*

State area. The region where we lived at the time was certainly not known as a culinary paradise, but there was one recipe that had passed down through generations of my mother's family, a baked bean dish that was different from other baked beans in other regions of the country. My mother was insistent that the end result be neither too sweet (molasses was an ingredient) nor overcooked. Lulu Brown, in

Mexico, New York—very near my wife's job site—began marketing a baked bean product virtually identical to our family recipe. I first saw her baked beans sold in bulk at a butcher's counter in a super-market. Grandma Brown's Baked Beans eventually became a familiar product and, probably, became the major employer in the village of Mexico. My mother bought them; her recipe was time-consuming and Grandma Brown's product not that expensive.

Move, however, we did, leaving those good jobs so I could attempt to become a geographer. The move was only three hundred miles, almost due south, to central Pennsylvania and Penn State University. Once we had driven thirty miles, I was in brand-new territory.

Three hundred miles does not seem like much, particularly in an era of interstate highways, but we decided to stop overnight in Elmira, New York, fewer than 150 miles from our starting point. At the time of our trip, *Elmira did not prominently advertise the fact that Mark Twain had made his summer home at Quarry Farm in Elmira.* The last time I was there, signs left no doubt that Twain had once lived there.

The following day we crossed the state border, entering Pennsylvania—the first time there for both of us. Soon thereafter we passed through *Williamsport, Pennsylvania, the home of Little League Baseball and the site of the annual Little League World Series.* This was a special thrill for me because my gym teacher eventually became the president of all of Little League, worldwide.

The landscape began to look different as we moved south of Williamsport; it would take years of geographic education before I leaned why. Eventually, we came to the city of Lock Haven, Pennsylvania, at which point we encountered what I can only describe as a parking lot for small airplanes. It turned out (at that time) that Lock Haven was home of the famous Piper Cub, the aircraft equivalent of the Model T Ford or the Volkswagen Beetle, that is, the most popular aircraft for general aviation. *Several of the Piper Cubs were yellow; the most common color for the plane—the specific color was "Lock Haven Yellow."*

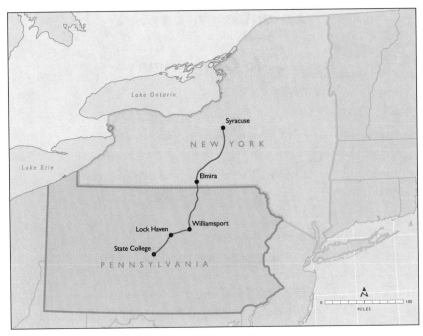

*Syracuse, New York, to State College, Pennsylvania*

We finally arrived in State College, Pennsylvania, the most delightful town we had even been in! An enormous amount was different. Driver's licensing, taxation, the passion associated with the volunteer fire department, the purchase and consumption of beer and other adult beverages, and especially the food. Things changed so much in only three hundred miles that, at times, it seemed like we had moved to a different country. No Grandma Brown's beans, but pearl tapioca and souse!

Dr. G. says: At the time, the legal age to consume alcoholic beverages was twenty-one in Pennsylvania but only eighteen in New York.

# *From Geography . . .*

# *. . . to Gastronomy*

~

### Food for Thought:

*"Part of the secret of success in life is to eat what
you like and let the food fight it out inside."*

—Mark Twain

~

### *Recipe for:*

Stovetop "Baked" Beans

# STOVETOP "BAKED" BEANS

*Serves 10–12*

I make these often and everyone loves them. They go well with roasted cuts of meat that have been cooked ahead and sliced for sandwiches—pork tenderloin on molasses brown bread or roast beef on hoagie rolls with a creamy coleslaw or herbed potato salad. It is a perfect take-along for potlucks and large family gatherings. You can indeed cook these in the oven if desired, or put them in a slow cooker, but I have found this the fastest and easiest way to deliver these beans to a hungry crowd.

## INGREDIENTS

I lb. small white or Great Northern beans, soaked overnight
½ lb. low-sodium bacon, cut into small pieces
I medium onion, chopped
6 cloves garlic, sliced thin
I cup brown sugar, packed
2 cups ketchup
6 tablespoons maple syrup
6 tablespoons dark molasses
¼ cup Worcestershire sauce
I tablespoon vanilla extract
Salt and pepper to taste

## MY METHOD

Drain soaked beans and pour them into a Dutch oven. Cover with water and bring to a boil. Reduce heat slightly so they do not boil over, and simmer until tender, about 45 minutes. You will have to test their "doneness" by tasting them. Don't let them get too mushy or they won't stand up to the sauce. Drain and reserve I cup of the cooking water. You can also use a pressure cooker to reduce energy and time for cooking the beans. Follow the manufacturer's instructions.

Using the same pot, sauté the bacon over medium heat until fat is rendered and bacon is browned and crisp. Remove with a slotted metal spoon onto a plate lined with paper towels to drain. Pour off all but 2–3 tablespoons of the bacon grease into your grease jar. Add in the onions and cook for 7–8 minutes. Add in garlic and cook, stirring, for another 3–4 minutes.

Reduce the heat to the lowest setting and add in the brown sugar. Stir constantly until it is fully dissolved and bubbling, about 5 minutes. Turn off heat.

Add in remaining ingredients, including the beans and reserved cooking water and mix well.

Turn the heat back on to medium and bring to a simmer. Reduce heat slightly and cook for 30 minutes, stirring often making sure to scrape the bottom of the pot. Serve hot. Enjoy!

# INDEX